HOW TO TALK TO GOD
When You Aren't Feeling Religious

CHARLES MERRILL SMITH
author of
How to Become a Bishop without Being Religious
When the Saints Go Marching Out
The Pearly Gates Syndicate

CHARLES MERRILL SMITH

WORD BOOKS, Publisher
Waco, Texas

HOW TO TALK TO GOD

When You Aren't Feeling Religious

How to Talk to God
When You Aren't Feeling Religious

Copyright © 1971 by Charles Merrill Smith

Printed in the United States of America
Library of Congress catalog card number: 74-175726

This is for Phil and Lois
relatives, but also good people
and valued friends

Contents

Foreword

Authors have an obligation to tell prospective purchasers what they will be getting if they do buy the book. Or what they are not getting.

Christian readers often look for books with a liberal slant or a fundamentalistic point of view. This book would be a poor investment for anyone seeking confirmation of his theological predisposition. I have been called a liberal, and I have been called a conservative—and neither is correct.

Nor should people seeking a well-packaged set of Christian answers buy this book. There are answers here, some of them quite positively stated. But there are more questions than answers.

My own conviction is that asking the right questions is more vital to the life of faith than arriving at a set of precise answers. The questions raised in these pages are real questions—real for me—because they are questions with which I have personally wrestled, and am still wrestling. Some of them have to do with faith and my personal life, others with how the Christian should look at the issues of the day which confront us, and still others with the Christian and how he relates to the church. Problems which bother me may leave you untroubled, but there must be millions of people who are bugged by the things which bug me. I'm not all that extraordinary.

About the format. These are not prayers. Prayers, trammeled

11

by our conscious or unconscious "religious" stance, leave out much that we really want to say. Too often, in our praying, we are guarded with God.

These, then, are more in the nature of communications directed toward God, uninhibited by the forms we deem appropriate to prayer. I find writing these communications a wonderful way to organize my own thinking. There is no reason why you can't try it for yourself.

On the chance that some people who have read my satirical works will read this book expecting more of the same, it should be made clear that this is not a satire. Satire depends, for its effectiveness, on the author pretending to believe the opposite of what he actually believes. Not so here. Like satire, there is some humor here—or at least I intended it so. Like satire, some of what you read here will irritate and needle you—again, it is intended. But this book is written "straight." It is how I see it.

Finally, I hope the book will be liberating to the person who has been raised, as I was, in the faith and in the church, but can no longer buy all the answers he was given in the process.

Most of us go through the trauma of discarding old answers, but we often feel guilty when we do it. Sometimes we are even afraid to articulate the questions we desperately need to ask. We want to go on being Christian, but we fear that probing our inherited faith will destroy our precarious hold on it.

Of course it will. But one has to let go in order to obtain a firmer grip. The good news I bring you, and the proposition on which these pages are based, is that the Christian faith is open-ended. It is valid, sufficient, and sustaining for even the people who must live out their lives in twentieth-century technological society. We just need to ask of it the right questions. The right questions are always the questions which really concern us.

This is good news indeed!

1

When Piety Isn't Sufficient

Dear God, Lord, Father, or Sir . . . I'm not certain, in the light of my subsequent remarks, just how to address You. When I'm talking to You in church, muttering the Lord's Prayer or joining in the General Confession, I follow holy protocol of course, but this is different. What I want to say now is no pious verbal ballet; it's the real thing. Also, I'm not feeling very religious at the moment, which perhaps requires an explanation so that You won't get me wrong.

You see, we American Christians, especially of the middle class (to which I belong), like to compartmentalize life. There is a time to work, we believe, and a time to play, and a time to pray. Perhaps You have noticed this. The proper time to pray, we think, is when we are in church, or during what the prayer manuals call "the quiet hour" or "the precious time" or something like that. The point is that we

15

are supposed to clear our thoughts and spirits of all the cares and intrusions of the world so that we can be in a truly devotional frame of mind. We can free the soul, so to speak, and talk to You properly.

Well, that's all right. I admit it does feel good to talk to You, along with fellow Christians, in the familiar and resonant language of the Prayer Book.

But it isn't enough for me. It is precisely the cares and intrusions of the world which I am supposed to shut out when talking to You that I want to talk about.

These cares and intrusions are the things that bother me, foul up my life, upset my digestion, baffle me, frustrate me, pilfer my peace of mind, ruin my good nature, and in general give me a pain. I feel like the psalmist when he said, "O Lord, how many are my foes! Many are rising against me." Only it isn't people that bug me so much as situations, problems, changing values, crumbling culture, rigid institutions, simple sappy solutions to incredibly complex dilemmas which are urged on me—things like that. I'm not so much paranoiac as puzzled.

Speaking of the psalms, I identify with those old boys who gave it to You straight—complaining, arguing, finding fault, and so on. Biblical scholars, as You no doubt know, call these conversations or monologues addressed to God "individual laments." If they could talk this way to You and get in the Bible with it, I ought to be able to lay it on the line too without being accused of irreverence. I don't intend to be irreverent. I just want to talk to You without the normal religious impediments to honesty, without it sounding like I'm talking in Old English script.

CHARLES MERRILL SMITH

16

Let me tell You a little about myself (I know You know all about me, even to the number of hairs on my head—which it isn't much of a job to count anymore, I'm afraid—but it will be good for me to recall my own cultural and spiritual heritage).

I was raised in a good Christian home, brought up in a standard brand (meaning large and socially acceptable) church, am married, and have a family. I've done very well careerwise if you measure by normal middle-class standards. I play golf, like a cocktail before dinner (even though I was brought up to believe this was sinful), am a registered Republican (I was taught that You vastly prefer the Republican Party to the Democratic Party.), and have been, at one time or another, a Kiwanian, a Rotarian, and a Lion.

I am, in short, a typical, moderately successful, American, middle-class, white, Anglo-Saxon, Protestant Christian. I'm also in what is graciously referred to as "the prime of life," which means I'm getting on.

You need to keep this background in mind in order to understand my subsequent laments, although let me hasten to say that I'm going to do more than just gripe. I have some very positive comments to make to You, too; this isn't all going to be negative.

The point is, these aren't prayers exactly. I'm not asking You to do anything about my concerns except maybe to help clear up some of my confusions. Mainly I just want You to listen to me. I wouldn't blame You if You didn't pay much attention to my religious-type talking in church and at religious meetings, places like that, because You've heard that kind of talk over and over and probably You get a little bored with it even if You are God.

But pay attention to what I have to say now, please, because I need to do this talking. It is a very deep spiritual need which I suspect I share with a lot of people (You would know about that, of course.), and doesn't it promise somewhere in the Scriptures that You are sufficient to every need?

Now back to how I should address You in these conversations. May I dispense with the "Dear Lords" and "God, our Father" type of salutations? Perhaps I should just address You as "Sir."

I know that You are more than my finite mind can conceive, but like all good American Christians I have been brought up to think of You as a rather grave and stern elderly statesman, something like Prime Minister Gladstone or General Douglas MacArthur, and I won't be able to free myself altogether from this concept.

Anyway, let's leave it at that and get on with the conversations.

CHARLES MERRILL SMITH

2

My Spiritual Options Are Shrinking

Eternal Spirit, Sir . . . In my previous remarks I indicated that I am at the moment a victim of spiritual dyspepsia. Reflection has convinced me that the condition is traceable to the shrinking of my spiritual options.

My personal spiritual history, in case it has slipped Your mind, is the same as for millions of white middle-class American Protestants past thirty. We all were taught to believe in God; of course Jesus was our savior, although preachers and Sunday school teachers were rather vague as to just how Jesus managed it. Some said it had to be done through an emotional experience receivable only— or at least best—at an "altar service" in a church of Protestant evangelical persuasion. Others favored following the life and teachings of Jesus as a sounder path to personal salvation.

Well, after a couple of trips to the altar, either in the throes of adolescent guilt feelings over sex (at that time largely fantasies rather than experience), or under the prodding of what the ungodly called "Christers" (spiritual bird dogs trained to spot a semipenitent sinner who needed only a bit of persuasion to push him forward), I abandoned the altar method of salvation.

If I were completely rational about all this I would shrug off these experiences, realizing that those anxious to save my boyish soul were well-intentioned people. But it left spiritual scars. I am, at this late day, revolted by the occasional television evangelist who exploits normal adolescent guilt feelings to get the kids to the altar and then counts them as "decisions for Christ," or nauseated when I hear one of those old altar-call hymns—sheer prejudice and Pavlovian reaction, I admit.

This left me the option of "following Jesus," which seemed a good option at the time, and still does, although my understanding of what it involves has shifted considerably during the years.

Other items in our spiritual history included the instruction that the Ten Commandments and the Sermon on the Mount (with priority to the commandments) combine to form a moral code which You expect us to follow literally; the identification of Christian culture and society with American middle-class white culture and society (which it was incumbent on us as Christians to export to Hindus, Buddhists, South Sea Islanders, and all "lesser breeds without the law" as Kipling put it, through our support of the foreign missions program of our denomination); the espousal of a mild anti-Roman Catholicism ("We don't want to be bigots, but we've got to keep the pope out of the White House."); a

CHARLES MERRILL SMITH

20

subdued anti-Semitism ("Jews will cheat you every time, and besides they were the ones who killed Christ.") ; the belief that sex and sin would be synonymous if it weren't for booze; that You always favored the United States in any war because U.S. culture and foreign policy were inevitably consistent with the divine will; that being a "good Christian citizen" meant conforming to the ideas of what a good Christian citizen is as understood by the leaders of church and community; and a lot of other stuff with which You are probably familiar so I won't go on with it.

Now God, or Sir, I'm not blaming You for the fact that this mishmash was foisted off on us in the name of God, Christ, Christian living, all that. It seems incredible that we swallowed it, but we did. In fact, You can still find people whose idea of Christian living approximates the above description.

But millions of us, I imagine, (although You would know more about that than I would) simply came down with spiritual indigestion. We can't buy it any more, even if we wanted to. I'm sure You won't hold it against us.

But when we reject this amalgam of culture, religion, and social values, what spiritual option is open to us?

As a group, we are still middle-class WASPs at heart. We aren't attracted to the nutty fringe of narrow sects preaching a loveless fundamentalism. Nor do many of us find much spiritual renewal in the psychedelic services of the youth culture, much as we may admire what they are trying to do.

Furthermore, many of us are turned off by the main-line, standard brand type of church. Actually, we were all brought up in this kind of church and are emotionally tuned to it. But most of them go right on putting out the same old religio-cultural pablum we found unappetizing a long time ago.

So what option is open to us?

We want to do our best to live out our faith in the world. Some of us have detached ourselves entirely from any community of faith and are going it alone. That's no good though, really. Others are splitting off from the organized church and forming their own small groups. This is more promising. These groups probably resemble the early church more nearly than does the congregation meeting in the pseudo-Gothic edifice at the corner of Main and Market streets. However, many of us would rather be a part of the congregation meeting at Main and Market streets, if we could only find that scene credible.

So what is our best spiritual option? We need help with this problem.

CHARLES MERRILL SMITH

22

3

My Children Upset Me

Father, Sir . . . Our previous conversation may have given You the idea that I am a bit of a rebel and look on our white middle-class folkways with a jaundiced eye. Actually, I rather fancy this self-image, but I'm afraid it is a fake. I'm much more firmly mortised into the traditional structure than I like to think.

How do I know? Because my children upset me when they blithely dismiss my religious and cultural values and insist on forging their own life-style, which is markedly different from mine.

Take the matter of security. I can't convince them that the wise course is to prepare yourself for a profession, get a job with a good company, and stay with it.

My son, who is now in his twenties, must have had by now more than twenty jobs. None of them were very good jobs, but they were a start. He chucked them all in rather short order. Quitting a rotten job, he says, is one of the truly exhilarating experiences life has to offer.

I just don't understand this attitude. My upbringing taught me that exhilaration comes from sticking to the job, no matter how punk, and doing it well. He thinks my attitude is stupid, and this upsets me.

My son also has a low opinion of higher education. He went to three colleges in three years, claimed that with the exception of a couple of courses all his classes were boring, irrelevant, totally out of touch with modern life, and a complete waste of time.

I tried to tell him that you can't expect all of life to be interesting and exciting. I tried to explain to him, sometimes patiently, sometimes in exasperation, that being bored and failing to learn anything important is a small price to pay in order to qualify for the job market. But he wouldn't listen. He said it was too high a price for him and refused to get a degree.

You can imagine how upset I was. We are all college people in my family. All good WASPs are thoroughly convinced that failure to obtain at least a bachelor's degree is giving hostages to economic fortune. I told my son (I'm afraid I yelled a little.) that I'd sunk a pot of money in his college work, such as it was, and he was blowing it. I demonstrated, conclusively, I thought, that he had no future, that he couldn't get a decent job. I predicted dire consequences.

So what does he do?

CHARLES MERRILL SMITH

24

He announces that he is going to be a writer. Now You can see, God, or Sir, that a boy who can't stick out four years of college isn't likely to stick at writing long enough to produce anything marketable.

That's what I thought, anyway. Anyone who has embraced WASP values as fondly as I have knows that anyone who can't keep at it and do a good job at distasteful tasks obviously can't do a good job of anything.

Well, he sat down and wrote a novel. If You have been following the publishing business, You are aware that it is next to impossible to get a first novel published these days. The market is glutted with first novels. My son, though, not only got his novel published without difficulty, he also sold it to the movies for a nice fat figure. As if this weren't enough, people who know about such things say he has a great future as a novelist and may well become one of America's major writers.

Naturally I'm as pleased as can be with his success. But I'm amazed, too. He flouted all the rules I believe in and came out fine. You can't help being upset when the traditional wisdom of our culture, passed down from generation to generation, is ignored by your own children and they seem to get along quite well without it. I mean, have I been wrong about all these mores and values?

The children do other things that upset me, too. I'm sure they smoke a little pot now and then, or at least have experimented with it—I don't want to know too much about this, so I don't inquire. They claim a joint of grass, as they call it, is just as pleasant and no more harmful than a cocktail before dinner. That upsets me.

HOW TO TALK TO GOD . . .

25

Then there is the matter of their rejection of the institutions of our society. For example, both my son and daughter were raised in the church, of course, but they won't go near it anymore. If they were hostile to the church I could understand it. A certain amount of hostility is to be expected toward any institution which has imposed restraints upon your conduct. But they aren't hostile toward it, merely indifferent. They say it is fine for people who like that sort of thing. But that it is in any way relevant (they like that word relevant), that it has any claim on them, that it is necessary to salvation, or that it is doing anything which needs doing, they reject. I argue with them, but I don't make a dent in their imperturbable indifference, and this upsets me.

Please don't think they are bad kids though. It is true that they use four-letter words, have little concern for middle-class grooming, are terribly suspicious of the business community, despise the military, think Spiro T. Agnew is a buffoon, and in many other ways violate the mores of their class and race. This may or may not upset You (I have been taught to believe that it does, but I might be wrong.), but if it does, do remember some things in their favor.

For example, they are fine, sensitive human beings. They exhibit affection, love, and concern for their mother and me. In fact, in this day when so many parents are complaining that they can't communicate with their kids, I have a relationship with my children that couldn't be better. This amazes me, and I have to say it is mostly due to them, not me. I surely don't agree with them much of the time, but I do get along with them, and for this I am grateful.

Also, they get upset at the injustice, the poverty, the indifference to human suffering we all know is present in our society—and this is definitely in their favor. I have always accepted these conditions as a part of the necessary order of things, but they say to accept them is unacceptable.

They are troubled by the wanton destruction of our environment, the desecration of Your good creation. They believe that personal growth, the appreciation of the world, and joy in living is more important than a successful career or making money. While some of these attitudes run counter to my values, I admit I find them attractive, and I hope You do too.

Maybe what really upsets me isn't my children (whom I love dearly), but the thought that they may be right about many things. If they are right, then I have been wrong, and anyone who suspects that he has been wrong is going to be upset.

My question is this: if I have been wrong, or if my values are no longer viable (I hate that word, but it means what I mean.), then how do I replace them? How do I get re-oriented?

4

Should I Feel Guilty over Enjoying Sex Tremendously?

Creator, Sir . . . At this moment I haven't a thing to complain of. The universe appears friendly, life is full of possibilities, my personal problems have receded.

I always feel like this just after—what euphemism should I resort to here?—a particularly grand coupling with my wife, and we have just finished. I hope You don't think it indelicate of me to mention the subject. Some people are awfully offended by any talk about sex, but I'm counting on You not to be offended.

Sometimes David Frost (You must know him. He's the son of an English Methodist minister, once did a little preaching himself, as a matter of fact, and now is host to television talk shows both here and in London.) will ask a guest on his show, "Why do you believe in God?" The answers are

28

usually about what you would expect—the beauty of the world, order in creation, sometimes because You allegedly got the believer out of a scrape or a hairy situation, that sort of thing.

If I am ever on the Frost show and he asks me, "Why do you believe in God?" I will answer with just one word. I'll say "Sex."

If, in this imaginary dialogue with David Frost, he presses me to amplify my answer, I'll say something like this: "There are many indications of God's existence, but for me nothing nails it down half so well as a superb sex experience. I might be persuaded that this collection of atoms called earth accidentally came together as a result of a cosmic bang. I could even imagine that the stars in their courses were hurled into position by a mindless force. But when I am locked to the body of the woman I love—when we are melded in tenderness, passion, and joy—I can't believe this amazing creation came about except by the hand of an intelligent, wise, compassionate creator. Nothing that is so much fun as sex could have been an unplanned accident of natural forces. No way."

That's what I'd say. You know, of course, that not everyone feels this way about sex. Once when I was a guest on a television talk show (the "Tonight" show starring Johnny Carson—You should catch it sometime, he's very entertaining) I did say something nice about sex and You should read the mail I got from religious-type folks! Such hostility!

Religious-type people, it seems, often have rather odd attitudes toward copulation. Some of them are convinced that when You created two sexes You maybe didn't exactly make a mistake (to think that would be blasphemy), but that this is the weakest part of creation and that You could have come up with a more acceptable arrangement if You had put Your mind to it. Others consider sexual activity as a sort of nasty necessity best disposed of with a minimum of fuss so that we can devote our time and energies to "higher things" (such as reading devotional literature, participating in church activities, and making money).

Let me make it clear that I don't feel guilty over enjoying sex as much as I do—at least I don't feel guilty at the conscious level. Heaven knows, of course, what a psychiatrist would find if he poked around in the recesses of my subconscious. Sometimes, though, I have a twinge or two of guilt because I don't feel guilty about all the fun I get out of sex.

You'd hardly believe the number of good Christian people I know who do feel guilty about enjoying sex, even with their husbands or wives. Actually, those of us who are more or less middle-aged were raised to be terrified of sex, especially if we were raised in the church—almost any church.

My first sex book (not counting the pornography we passed around surreptitiously at school) was *What Every Young Boy Should Know,* written by some Lutheran preacher (It sold by the millions, so he made a bundle.). Parents gave it to their adolescent sons, content that, authored by an eminent divine, it would give them the straight Christian goods on sex.

What it did was to scare the hell out of us. What I remember most about it was that it contained fervid descriptions of the horrors awaiting masturbators. None of us gave up masturbation, of course, but we learned to feel guilt and terror over it. (If I remember correctly, this same preacher also wrote

CHARLES MERRILL SMITH

What Every Young Girl Should Know. He knew he was on to a good thing, evidently. I don't know how he scared the girls, but I'll bet he did.)

Well, Sir, you can't have it dinned into you by preachers, teachers, community attitudes, etc. that sex is an expression of our "lower nature" (I recently heard a sociologist, a Ph.D. yet, use that very term on a TV panel discussing the sexual revolution, honest.) without accumulating some hang-ups on the subject.

And, oh boy, do we have hang-ups!

Parents are petrified over the possibility that their teenage daughters will get pregnant or that their sons will contract a "social disease" or have to get married.

As a society, we make marriage economically unfeasible until kids are well into their twenties, but insist that they postpone sexual experience until it is blessed by the clergy, which seems a bit unrealistic.

We believe it is fine for our children to witness murder, sadism, all sorts of bloody brutality on the tube, but rigidly exclude from their impressionable gaze more than a hint that a man and a woman often end up in bed together.

Bob Hope, the master of the suggestive, double-entendre joke, is considered one of our greatest living Americans. Lenny Bruce, however, who employed blunt Anglo-Saxon words to talk about sex in his comedy routines, was harried, hounded, persecuted, and jailed the last years of his brief life. I'm not trying to make a case for Lenny so that You will let him into heaven if he has gone to the other place. I'm certain You are completely just in these matters plus

HOW TO TALK TO GOD . . .

31

also compassionate. But doesn't this seem ridiculous to You?

Also, while I don't want to get into politics right now, there is our vice-president who is making a name for himself as a persecutor of permissiveness. He fulminates against obscenity-using, sexually uninhibited young people, which is O.K. if that is how he feels. Yet he belongs to a group whose members call one another at all hours to share the latest dirty jokes. It isn't that I'm trying to say he's a bad guy. The point is that he is an excellent example of our national sex hangups.

Now Creator, Sir, it seems to me that if the Old Testament is right and You made everything, and that You looked upon it and saw that it was good—all of it—then this includes sex, right? If so, then our traditional attitudes toward sex are pretty sick, right?

On the other hand, if the Greek philosophers were right when they divided man into body and spirit and said what we have is the good spirit trapped in the bad body, then the traditional churchly attitude that sex belongs to the lower, inferior part of our nature is right. It troubles me some that this Greek philosophy is reflected here and there in the New Testament. Since I have always thought highly of the New Testament, it is understandable that now and then I feel guilty about not feeling guilty over enjoying sex so much.

In short, if the Hebrews were right, then my relish for sex makes me in tune with creation and the divine will. However, if the Greeks were right, then it makes me a dirty old, or rather middle-aged, man.

So I think I'll stick with the Hebrews when it comes to my attitude toward creation.

CHARLES MERRILL SMITH

32

I'll admit that sex causes a multitude of problems. I'm sophisticated enough to know that many people express their sexuality in pretty kinky ways. But I have a hunch that the problems and the kinks are not attributable to a faulty creation. I'll bet they can be traced to unhealthy cultural conditioning. In other words, it isn't Your fault, it's ours.

What I really wanted to say in this conversation was to express my deep and eternal gratitude for Your idea of creating two sexes.

Some people hold that there won't be any sex in heaven, but that's hard for me to imagine. Without sex how could it be heavenly?

5

My Training Conflicts with My Inclinations

Good Sir . . . You are supposed to be the source of all wisdom and righteousness, and the wisdom to know what is right is what I need at the moment.

If You have noticed the way in which we middle-class white Christians are trained, You know that we learn early and are never allowed to forget that You supposedly approve highly of the man who works long and hard at whatever his job may be even when he would rather be doing something else. This is a fundamental principle, and my generation has its very bones impregnated with this doctrine.

Now, while I never have been overly fond of hard work and long hours, I guess I am in thrall to this ethic.

For example, I'm often inclined to goof off. I get impulses

to take a walk through the woods in autumn, watch the World Series on a weekday, prowl the city streets just people-watching, go shopping with my wife, sit around for hours talking with friends, and any number of other delightful but profitless ways of passing the time.

I often follow my inclinations, but my enjoyment of these enjoyable pursuits is inhibited by a ubiquitous nagging conviction that I really ought to be working. Most of my contemporaries and peers have the same problem. That's why recreations such as golf and bowling are so popular with us—even when having fun we need to keep score.

Answer these questions, please:

Do You really like me better when I'm plugging away than when I'm dogging it?

If Jesus is my example, then why didn't he keep office hours?

Do you disapprove of hippies? I suppose You do. They toil not, neither do they spin. They wear some pretty weird get-ups, and they don't wash much. All good WASPs, of which I guess I'm one, disapprove of hippies because they don't take our cultural codes, mores, folkways, etc. seriously.

Don't worry; I couldn't ever be one. I've been so preconditioned that I actually like our cultural patterns.

But sometimes I envy the hippies their carefree enjoyment of the world without feeling guilty that they aren't getting ahead or making any money or putting in time on the job.

Does this make me a bad guy?

HOW TO TALK TO GOD . . .

35

6

I Worry Too Much

Heavenly Father, Sir . . . Though I think of myself as a
Christian and therefore believe I ought to obey Jesus' in-
junction to take no thought for the morrow, what I shall eat
and what I shall drink, and all that, I'm still one of the
world's great worriers. If there was an Olympic competition
category for worrying, I would make the team easy, maybe
be captain.

You should see my list of worries.

Most of my life I worried like sixty about making it—career
advancement, professional recognition, the symbols and
trappings of success—the kind of stuff most of us middle-
class upward strivers worry about. I didn't worry about my
health, was even willing to undermine it, burn the candle at
both ends, if I could just make it.

36

Now that I've made it to my own satisfaction (have done far better than I ever thought I would, really), I don't worry about getting ahead, but I do worry about my health.

Will my prostate hold out as long as I do?

Will I have a stroke and be a vegetable for years?

Will cancer's quiet tentacles clutch some vital organ and I won't know it until too late?

Will that old gall bladder trouble, dormant for years now, flare up and lay me low?

If I play a brisk game of badminton, will I overtax myself and blow a gasket?

You should see the pills I take! It isn't easy to remember which one to gulp when. I think hypochondriacs are ridiculous, comical really, but I'm in a fair way to becoming one.

I worry about money. I fret over my children. I conjure up spectacles of bloody crashes whenever I drive anywhere. In those moments when I'm not worried I feel like I ought to be worrying about something and would be if I could only remember what it is.

Perhaps my fretful nature accounts for my admiration for Jesus' teaching that living life as fully as possible one day at a time is the only way to live. How I envy the people who can manage to live that way. And how I try!

I'm familiar, of course, with all the pious admonitions on the subject of worry—have even handed them out myself from time to time.

HOW TO TALK TO GOD . . .

Trust in God—that's a common one. And I do. But that doesn't mean that You will protect me against the normal vicissitudes of living, or ward off the ills human flesh is heir to.

Think positively! That's Norman Vincent Peale's line. I've done my share of poking fun at it. You recognize, I'm sure, that Dr. Peale often makes incredible claims for it, and as a substitute for religious faith, it is pretty shallow. However, I've come to believe that there is something in it. It is, after all, consistent with the biblical doctrine of creation. That is, if this is Your world and You are the author of my existence, and You think it is a good world and a good life, then my only godly option is to be an optimist.

You'll forgive me, I hope, that existence without worry doesn't come easy for me.

Intellectually I agree 100 percent with Jesus' teaching on the subject. It's my emotional structure that keeps me from living that way. Maybe the fault is in my genes. Or maybe my middle-aged chemistry is responsible. Or, heaven forbid, encroaching senility. Sometimes what preachers ascribe to lack of faith is more the result of hormonal imbalance or vitamin deficiency than of theological inadequacy.

I expect this is the case with me and millions like me. I hope that's all it is. If so, we need to improve our diet and get more exercise. Maybe the doctor has some shots he could give us that would help.

Also, like Avis, we should try harder, I expect.

CHARLES MERRILL SMITH

7

Is the Christian Life Like a Baseball Game?

Omniscient Sir . . . You may not be very well acquainted with Leo Durocher, although he frequently utters Your name (as well as the name of Jesus Christ), but not, I'm afraid, in the context of prayer or theological discussion. Leo is the highly successful manager of professional baseball teams. He is noted for his acerbic and profane dialogues with umpires, and for his thorough grasp of the game.

Leo once said that "baseball is a game of inches."

Now, Sir, if you don't happen to be a baseball fan, that doesn't mean much. But what he meant was that the difference between an easy out and a sharp single is often whether the shortstop can get his glove on the ball or whether it is an inch or so beyond his frantic grasp; the difference between safely stealing second base (Stealing is not considered unethical in baseball.) or being tagged out is getting your foot on the bag a split second before the ball arrives; the difference between a home run or a long foul depends on which side of the foul pole it landed.

In short, it is a very fine line which separates failure from success.

My question: is this an apt parable for living the Christian life?

If You should drop in on the services of a big city church some Sunday (which perhaps You do), a church where the congregation considers itself theologically literate and the preacher has a Ph.D from Edinburgh or maybe Union Theological Seminary, You are likely to hear talk about " a lived-out faith," or "confronting contemporary society from the stance of faith," and similar felicitous phrases.

The village variety of preacher is more likely to speak in less sophisticated theological language about "living the Christian life seven days a week instead of just on Sunday." As nearly as I can make out, though, they are saying the same thing.

But how do I go about it?

Is there a line which separates Christian living from unchristian living, like the third base line which, if I hit to the right of it (or even plunk on it) I'm in fair territory, and if I hit to the left of it (even by a fraction of an inch) it's a foul?

Baseball is a game of rules. It has a rule to cover every conceivable situation. You can't score unless you are scrupu-

CHARLES MERRILL SMITH

40

lous about observing the rules. Is this analagous to playing the Christian game?

We middle-class white, Anglo-Saxon Christians have been taught that this is how it is. The sports metaphor for the Christian life is very popular with television preachers and big-name evangelists. We are always being exhorted to "hit a home run for Jesus" or "score a touchdown for Christ."

But some of us—a lot of us, I suspect—are beginning to wonder if we don't need a new metaphor.

One difficulty with playing the Christian game is that there is no substantial agreement among Christians on the rules. The Baptists play by one set of rules, the Episcopalians by another, the Presbyterians make up Presbyterian rules, etc., ad infinitum.

This can be pretty confusing.

You can, for example, keep the Episcopalian rules and be considered a winner, but by Baptist rules you are a loser. What kind of a ball game is that?

The Presbyterians, who play by rules laid down by John Calvin (Is he in heaven with You? If he is, I'm not sure I want to go there.), say the game is entirely in the hands of the umpire.

For Presbyterians (and other Calvinists) it's like that story about the umpire who called a low outside pitch a strike. The catcher turned to him in amazement and said, "I thought that pitch was pretty low and outside."

HOW TO TALK TO GOD . . .

41

"It was," the umpire replied.

"Then why is it a strike?" the catcher asked.

"Because I called it a strike," the umpire said—and that ended that.

You are the umpire in the Calvinistic Christian game, of course, and no one can object to that. What I can't swallow is the Calvinist who then tells me exactly how You call the game. How does he know?

Another problem is that many of the rules we are supposed to play by are at best petty and at worst downright ridiculous.

Are you upset if I imbibe a martini (very dry—just a whiff of vermouth)? The Methodists and Baptists (Southern) say You are.

Does it make You furious when people practice birth control by artificial devices or chemicals? The Roman Catholic rules assure us that it does.

Will You lock the doors of heaven against me if I haven't been baptized by Trinitarian formula or completely submerged? Several sects claim that You will.

Will I lose the game if I fail to affirm the Nicene Creed? Plenty of Christian ball clubs (if I may be permitted to expand the metaphor) have that in their bylaws.

It is my observation that Christians who insist you have to play the Christian game by the rules tend to select only those rules they happen to like, call them authentic, then discard the others.

CHARLES MERRILL SMITH

42

I was on this television talk show (it was the "Irv Kupcinet Show" out of Chicago, well worth watching sometime when You aren't too busy) with the Reverend Billy James Hargis. (You must know Billy James, the famous Oklahoma evangelist. He says he is one of the few remaining truly prophetic voices, and he really lays down the rules of the Christian game.)

One of the other guests was a lay supporter of Billy James, a rather grim-looking old millionaire whose name escapes me at the moment. This chap was berating me for being an ethical relativist, and I said, "Yes, I am an ethical relativist, isn't everyone?"

No sir, by George, he said, he wasn't. He believed literally in the Ten Commandments as absolute, every one of them. So then I said, "Well, inasmuch as one of the commandments says 'Thou shalt not kill,' then you are of necessity a pacifist, aren't you?"

Sir, you should have seen him explode! He got so red I thought he was going to have a stroke right there on camera. No sir, he wasn't any sneaky, comsymp pacifist, etc., etc., etc., he yelled at me.

"Then," I said, quite logically I thought, "you believe in the nine commandments."

Well, he was so enraged as to be speechless—at least he didn't speak to me again, even when the show was over and the guests were saying good-by to one another (Billy James, who had gone after me pretty hard on the program, was very friendly.).

My point is, how can you have much of a ball game if everyone insists on using only the rules he likes?

HOW TO TALK TO GOD . . .

43

Actually, I don't like the metaphor of a game for the Christian life. I'm a hot sports fan, which I hope is O.K. with You, but the Christian life doesn't appeal to me as a game.

For one thing, a game is played under rigid, carefully controlled conditions, and even then they have trouble making the rules cover every contingency.

Like, for example, the time when someone laid a perfect, slow-rolling bunt down the third base line and Pepper Martin, a third baseman of unsurpassed skills, saw that he didn't have a prayer (if You will pardon the expression) of throwing the man out. Martin was rather inventive, so he quickly dug a little trench with his spikes right in the path of the ball. The ball trickled into the trench in fair territory and then, as Martin had designed, trickled right into foul territory. The other team screamed bloody murder, but there wasn't any rule to cover the situation and Martin got away with it. (There's a rule now, of course, and anyway you couldn't dig a trench in the artificial grass infields they use today.)

So if it is tough to make enough rules fast enough to anticipate every situation in a ball game, how can anyone expect to figure out in advance the endless novel situations which arise in real life?

Then a ball game, after all, is make believe. You play it under artificial and circumscribed conditions, and though you pretend the outcome is important, any sensible person knows that it doesn't make much difference.

If the Christian life is just a game with made-up rules, then I don't want to play. The agony and the ecstasy of life, the pain and joy and frustration and fun and disappointments and possibilities of living are real, and how it comes out is important. So it isn't very appropriate, it seems to me, to play it like a baseball game.

Maybe our best metaphor for the Christian life is the one favored by the early church. They thought of it as a long, perilous sea voyage through uncharted waters, as You know.

I like that. The sea is large, and exciting possibilities await the voyager. He starts with a conviction about his journey, its direction, its ultimate purpose—but no precise map. However, along the way there will be signs and clues (like the floating branch Columbus found) which will indicate either the need for a new direction or confirm the course he is on.

Is this how it is, Sir?

The way I feel now I am going to ignore the cascade of confusing counsel on the Christian life which is about to engulf me, which wants to hem me in, squeeze me down, narrow my options, force my existence into confining cultural molds— and set sail for some unseen destination of the spirit in the expectation that the voyage as well as the goal will be a glorious experience.

I hope You approve.

8

Check Me Out on This Fable

Source of All Wisdom, Sir . . . We Christians have been
taught that when it comes to salvation it isn't what one knows
but what one feels that saves us. One doesn't need to know
what the Bible says nor what Jesus taught. We can be devoid
of any coherent theology, so we are told, just so long as our
heart is right.

This annoys me.

Let me hasten to say that I don't subscribe to the theory that
knowledge alone will save us. To do so would make me a
Gnostic, and Gnosticism was the first Christian heresy, and
so far as I know it is still a heresy.

However, if You created us, You created our minds and presumably expected us to use them, as You were not frivolous

when creating (with the possible exception of the giraffe). It seems to me, therefore, sinful to preach a doctrine which exalts the heart and downgrades the mind.

I'm not always certain I'm right about this. So in order to clarify my own thinking, plus have a little fun, I have written this fable. It is more in the literary tradition of James Thurber than it is of Jesus, but it is a parable of sorts. Would You be so good as to read it and check me out on it?

THE HARE WHOSE HEART WAS IN THE RIGHT PLACE

There was this Bear who was ordinarily pleasant, good natured, and friendly. He was well liked by all the animals and was much in demand as a party guest or dinner companion or fourth at bridge.

One day when the animals were just sitting around talking politics and religion and existentialism, a Coon said, "Bear, you aren't taking much part in this discussion."

"Apart from the fact that I don't dig Kierkegaard," the Bear replied, "I've been feeling poorly of late."

"Better see a doctor," the Horse said. "I know a very fine doctor of veterinary medicine who has treated me many times and always successfully. Recently, when I had an extremely severe case of horse colic, he prescribed a most efficacious dose, and then put me on a diet which has prevented any recurrence of the condition. I recommend him without reservation."

"How's he with the knife?" asked a Dog who had had several minor operations and considered himself something of an authority on surgery.

"One of the best," replied the Horse. "He corrected a serious condition for an uncle of mine slick as a whistle."

"If I may be permitted a question," the Hare said, "is this doctor's heart in the right place?"

"What's that got to do with it?" asked the Badger, who was suspected of being an agnostic and thus was not highly regarded in the community.

"Why, it has everything to do with it, everything," the Hare said, as if only an ignoramus could fail to grasp this.

"How so?" asked the Badger skeptically.

"Because it's what you have in here that makes all the difference," the Hare said, tapping his chest. "Now take me. I think I can say without being immodest that I have achieved an enviable position in life—top of my profession, bank account, solid investments, respected in the community, etc. Of course, I have worked hard, lead a sober life, and have a good character. But it is mostly due to the fact that my heart's in the right place. Think with your heart and you won't go wrong."

"If I were you, Bear," the Hare continued, before anyone could interrupt him, "I'd find a doctor whose heart is in the right place. I happen to know one, use him all the time myself. I'll be glad to introduce you to him."

"My doctor took his training at a reputable school of veterinary medicine," the Horse said with considerable force. "He has a thorough knowledge of the field, and an extensive library to which, if in doubt over a diagnosis, he can turn for confirmation or further information. What are your doctor's credentials?"

CHARLES MERRILL SMITH

48

"Oh, if it comes to that, he took a couple of correspondence courses from some mail-order college of medical and divine science," the Hare said, "and has a very handsome diploma to prove it. But the important thing is that he has faith."

"Faith in what?" asked the Badger, who made a habit of raising troublesome questions and saying things that disturbed people.

"Oh, faith in himself, faith in the Big Animal in the Sky," the Hare said. "It isn't important what you have faith in— just so you have faith."

"I feel worse," the Bear said at this point, "I'd better get to some kind of a doctor."

Here a big argument took place among the animals as to which doctor Bear ought to see. The Fox, who was a politician, insisted that a vote be taken because the majority ought always decide what was right and what was wrong. So the animals voted, and unfortunately the vote was a tie.

"The thing to do," the Fox insisted, "is for Bear to see both doctors. The animals have spoken."

So the Horse took Bear to his doctor who quickly diagnosed the trouble as an obstruction of the colon and recommended immediate surgery to be followed by a strict diet and regular exercise. He also took some pains to explain the Bear's insides to the Bear so that his patient would know why he should do what he should do.

Then the Hare, whose heart was in the right place, took Bear to his doctor, whose heart was also in the right place. This doctor hardly bothered to examine Bear, and right off said

HOW TO TALK TO GOD . . .

49

what Bear should do to alleviate his distress was to think good thoughts, have faith, and then his heart would be in the right place and everything would be O.K.

"But the other doctor, who is a well-informed man, said I needed an operation," Bear protested.

"You certainly wouldn't put the opinion of mere knowledge above the opinion of faith, would you?" the doctor asked contemptuously.

"Hear, hear," said the Hare.

When the animals heard about the two diagnoses, they had a big argument as to whose advice Bear should follow.

"Bear should go along with my doctor," the Hare insisted. "Faith is more important than knowledge, and besides the way of the heart is so much easier."

"I'm all for faith," the Horse countered, "but it should be informed by knowledge. My doctor is a man of faith, too. He knows he isn't God, and he knows how much he doesn't know. But he has made an effort to inform himself, and he possesses the knowledge which can save Bear."

"In medical matters one man's opinion is as good as another's," Hare said.

So the Hare whose heart was in the right place carried the day and the animals voted that Bear should follow the counsel of Hare's doctor. They also passed a vote of censure against the Horse and called him an intellectual and other dirty names.

CHARLES MERRILL SMITH

When Bear died three days later, Hare said piously, "It is the will of the Big Animal in the Sky," and they gave Bear the finest funeral ever.

MORAL: *When you need the knowledge that can save you, it's best to get it from the horse's mouth.*

9

I Don't Know How to Pray

Great Listener, Sir . . . If there is any one thing which baffles me about the Christian life it is how to pray to You.

All the preachers I have ever heard, all the Sunday school teachers I ever had, plus prestigious people such as Jane Russell, Bobby Richardson, Governor Maddox, and J. Edgar Hoover urge and recommend that I ought to pray to You a lot. So I've read stacks of books on prayer and have even gone out of my way to hear what we sometimes refer to as "prayer experts" tell me the ins and outs of praying, but none of this has helped me much. My trouble is that I can spot so many problems in their solutions. So I have some questions.

First, though, let's agree that public prayers in worship services are mostly designed for the spiritual benefit of the

52

congregation. That's fine with me. When the minister has taken the trouble to gather up the problems, aspirations, disappointments, joys, longings, etc. common to us all, and states them to You in a succinct and, hopefully, a nonunctuous voice, then I am moved and—for a little while at least —spiritually healthier. Pastors, although they seldom realize it, do more for the congregation through a well-thought-out, simply uttered, pastoral prayer than through the sermon.

When it comes to my private prayers, though, I am confused. What I need to know is what I have to know when I play golf—what are the rules, where are the out-of-bounds markers, what is par praying, etc.

For example, Sir, is it legal to pray for the success of my own plans and ambitions, or is this praying in the rough?

Somewhere I saw a prayer prayed by a successful Christian businessman who has put together a giant motel chain. His prayer asked You to make this a big year for him, pile on the profits, turn his motel chain into the biggest business of the kind in the whole world (He was about to go international with it, I believe.). He qualified the prayers in accepted humble fashion by adding "if it be Thy will," but the import of the orison was that You could hardly disagree with his wishes, he being such a good pal of Yours, going to church every Sunday, paying 10 percent of his profits (after taxes, of course) to the church, and other godly causes.

What I want to know is, did he belt this one right down the middle of the religious fairway, or did he hook it into a theological sand trap? Do You give priority and fast service to good guys? He is a good guy, I suppose, being a practicing Christian who doesn't smoke or drink (although he sells hooch in his motels because you can hardly find a traveling salesman to stay in a place without a bar, and everyone knows how the hotel and motel business needs the salesman trade).

Personally, I would very much like to believe that if I pay attention to You, You will pay attention to me. It would be awfully nice if I could count on Your cooperation to bring my plans and ambitions to fulfillment. It would surely give me a decided advantage over the nonreligious who are competing with me. I mean, with You backing me how could I miss?

But I just can't believe it. This concept of prayer would make You like Mayor Daley, who of course listens to the petitions and fulfills the wishes of a faithful ward heeler a lot quicker than he does the requests of some lazy or rebellious party worker. I just can't believe You are like Mayor Daley.

Let's say it isn't quite legitimate for me to pray for my own selfish desires, then is it O.K. to pray for the well-being of my family and friends?

Most of us who pray at all pray for our loved ones. Could I pray for the recovery of a sick friend and expect You not only to listen but to do something about it? I always do when the need arises, but sometimes the friend recovers and sometimes he doesn't. How do I figure that? I know the standard answer—"God always answers prayer, but sometimes He says no." But that is actually a cop out. It doesn't tell me a thing I need to know.

I have also had X number of prayer experts tell me that I ought to pray for my own spiritual improvement, strength to resist temptation, courage to cope with the tragedies and traumas of life which assault us all from time to time. These experts assure me that this kind of praying is not only theologically approved but always brings home the bacon. But this is another cop out. I don't need an expert to tell me that if I approach my life and its problems with a sincere desire to be a better person and a wish to be courageous in the face of adversity, that I probably will show improvement and cope more adequately. This comes under the heading of psychology, not prayer.

I could be wrong, but it appears to me that the kind of praying I do hinges on two questions: (1) Do You ever interfere, in a specific instance, in the natural order of Your universe? (2) Do You want us to feel and act dependent on You for the solution of our mortal, day-to-day problems?

I confess I don't know the answer to either of these questions. I would guess that the answer to the first question is "yes, but not often," and that the answer to the second question is "no."

If my guesses are correct, then the whole novena and shrine and holy medal and amulet business would go out the window, which would cause not only some economic hardship to the religious hustlers who push these items but severe emotional stress to millions of good, credulous Christians who no doubt gain much comfort and spiritual sustenance from believing that the answer to question number one is "yes, if you go to God through proper channels or if you are a person pleasing to Him. Or if you know the spiritual button to push, He will always interfere for your benefit," and that the answer to question number two is "yes, life is too big for us without leaning on the Everlasting Arms."

Please don't get me wrong, Sir. I'm not putting down people who believe this way. After all, what do I know that they don't know? But my mind doesn't work this way. Even though I would like it if I could believe that You would extend me special protection and care if I asked You in the correct manner, and that in other ways I qualified for special blessings, I can't believe it. I'd rather know the uncomfortable truth than live by a comforting illusion.

So, until I hear from You on the subject, I'll just go on sending up prayers of thanksgiving for the privilege of being alive in Your good creation, paeans of joy for the gifts of sight and hearing and feeling, appreciation for sunshine and food and friendship and sex, and praise for Jesus Christ who helps me make sense out of life.

I hope You will consider this adequate.

CHARLES MERRILL SMITH

10

Is the Church Like a 1932 Duesenberg?

Supreme Being, Sir . . . Is it a matter of concern in heaven that the churches, all of which claim to be operating in Your interests and in the name of Jesus Christ, are having a tough time of it these days?

Since Vatican II the Roman Catholic branch has been coming apart at the seams. Communiques from the Vatican, in case You haven't been reading them lately, seldom call us to faith, love, unity, and the other good ideas the church is supposed to promote. Rather, they are one continuous moan about priests dropping out (I thought the pope was a little hostile when he compared them to Judas, didn't You?), the slump in religious vocations, the indifference of the faithful, the failure of Catholic Christians to obey the authority of the church (especially the light-hearted attitude of Catholics toward the Vatican's edicts on birth control), and many other mutterings of a similar type.

The world's image of Paul VI is, I'm afraid, of a brilliant, lonely, confused man who seems to have little concept of the cultural, moral, and emotional currents which are battering the lives of people in the outside world.

The Protestant Churches aren't in any better shape, although instead of blowing up dramatically like the Roman branch they are sort of petering out. It's kind of sad, really, to see the way the churches stumble around trying to be "relevant," meaning trying to find a way to attract new business in an age which doesn't take the churches seriously.

Some of the churches, of course, refuse to budge one iota from what they say is the faith once delivered to the saints. They call themselves fundamentalists and claim to make no concessions to the modern world or secular culture. I think it's funny, sort of, that the most successful of these churches which denounce a modern world-view, secularism, scientism, etc. are the ones which employ up-to-date advertising and public relations methods, use the modern, scientific media of radio and television, and even tape prayers which one can hear by dialing a number.

Oddly, or maybe not so oddly when you come to think about it, the strict, fundamentalistic, theologically narrow churches are getting more than their fair share of the church trade these days. Perhaps it's because a good many people are looking for something they believe is changeless to cling to in a changing world.

The liberal churches, which have had a long and successful run, are really in trouble. They have always gone in for enlightenment, improving the social order, things like that. To my mind they have a fine record of liberating the Bible from the steely clutches of dogmatic, literal interpreters, and

CHARLES MERRILL SMITH

58

of keeping alive the Christian witness of the brotherhood of man when no one else was much interested in doing it.

But, let's face it, the world isn't concerned any more with the liberal versus the literal interpretation of the Bible (although I do want to talk to You about this a little later on in our conversations). And in a time when the experts, the smartest men we have, don't really know how to put our fractured social order back together, who is going to listen to liberal preachers tell them how?

I have a theory as to why the churches are in trouble, and I'd like Your reaction.

My theory has two parts. First, I believe the churches are asking themselves the wrong question. The question the churches ask themselves, although they would hate to admit it, is, "How can the institution of the church be saved?" This is what they have in mind when they talk about "renewal in the church" and "new life in the church," and other phrases of the same flavor.

The right question the church should be asking is, "How can the church exercise its authentic ministry to the world today?" Although the churches think they are asking this question, they aren't, because an honest answer might be, "First, rid yourself of your present structures, ecclesiastical bric-a-brac, useless and expensive hierarchical institutionalism, your dated cultus, everything you have been hoarding so carefully, then you will be free to make fresh, vital approaches to the true ministry of the church." Now I ask You, Sir, what institution wants to hear an answer like that? Who is going to vote himself out of a job?

The second part of my theory is that the world is just plain bored with the church.

It isn't against the church any more than it is against the Masonic order or the Rotary club. It just considers the church and the Masons and Rotary on the periphery of life. They aren't where the action is, if You will permit me to use that dreadful cliché.

That's bad. The church can survive, and has survived, hostility. It can thrive under persecution. It can live underground. But boredom can kill it pretty easy.

Even though I've been hung-up on the church all my life, I have to admit, Sir, that, objectively viewed, it is rather boring. The church built its program around the Sunday morning show it puts on. I'm not trying to be nasty, honest, but there is an accurate analogy between Sunday services and show business. Any occasion which includes music and speaking and seeks to involve the minds and emotions of those who attend has to be produced and staged.

The trouble is that the church, except in rare instances, doesn't put on a very good show by today's standards. One can get a lot better music on his hi-fi. Speakers more entertaining and enlightening than most preachers are available at the flick of a dial. Fewer and fewer people care to drag themselves out of bed to sing hymns written from a premodern world-view and, apart from the nostalgia they create in some of us older types, have no particular merit.

On top of this, young people are bored with old-fashioned, homiletically sound preaching—the kind of preaching I go for. On the other hand, the older people who do like such preaching are offended by the "with it" style of the younger clergy. Once in awhile one. walks into a church on Sunday morning where there is a quality of aliveness, vitality, a something-important-is-happening-here atmosphere, but not often.

CHARLES MERRILL SMITH

It isn't for me to advise heaven as to what it should do about it, but if, Sir, You are thinking of sending down a revelation on the subject of ecclesiastical reform, I'd like to make a suggestion or two as to what the revelation should contain.

My conviction is that the churches, as they are now organized, have had it. They are like a 1932 Duesenberg. A 1932 Duesenberg was a fine automobile. It was, and still is for that matter, a handsome automobile. It was comfortable to ride in. Mechanically it was way ahead of the times. One took pride in being a Duesenberg owner.

But they were expensive to buy. The upkeep was horrendous. And they were awfully big. Cheaper makes, smaller, better suited to the purpose for which a car is designed, drove the Duesenberg out of business.

Oh, there are a few Duesenbergs left, and a person can buy one if he has the price (which is substantially more than they cost when new). A Duesenberg today is a status symbol, an expensive toy. Duesenberg owners are like an esoteric cult —devoted, filled with spiritual pride, finicky about the care of their possession. But Duesenbergs are not used for the purpose for which they were designed, which was to transport people from one place to another.

What I am trying to say is, what does an army of paid ecclesiastical bureaucrats such as are housed at the Vatican or occupy offices at any denominational headquarters have to do with the church of God? Isn't the sight of an imposing church building on every downtown corner, each proclaiming to minister in the name of him who prayed that they all might be one, a sort of sick joke? What is the connection

HOW TO TALK TO GOD . . .

61

between catching the Sunday morning religious show and the gathered community of faith?

It seems to me, Sir, that the churches as we know them are afflicted with the Duesenberg psychology. They assume that somehow people can be persuaded to continue paying Duesenberg prices for their religion, even though the churches—while costing a bundle—don't do the job for which they were designed any more, at least not very well.

My suggestion is to let the people who want Duesenberg religion and are willing to pay for it go right on playing with their expensive Christian toy. After all, it's a free country, and they can't hurt anybody very much. But please send a revelation to some new Amos or Isaiah to call the community of faith to its true vocation, which is best summed up, it strikes me, in the traditional description of the Christian ministry as "a cure of souls."

And please include instructions to the professional clergy—but no, that's enough for now. I'll make this the subject of my next communication.

CHARLES MERRILL SMITH

62

11

Is the Professional Clergyman Obsolete?

Kindly Sir . . . As You know, I hope, I spent thirty years as a parish pastor. I'm still a card-carrying clergyman, although no longer practicing my former profession. I didn't get kicked out or anything like that. I suppose I could still get a parish if I'd trim my hair a little and buy a white shirt.

But I have a feeling that the professional clergyman is obsolete, which is why I was about to say when our last talk ended to please include instructions to the professional clergy in the new revelation about the church I hope You are going to give us. It is my conviction that You ought to instruct the clergy to lay off all the techniques of salvation they are currently practicing and ponder the possibilities in a genuine cure of souls.

What's happened, Sir, as I'm sure You know, is that these

guys have somehow confused salvation with the right connection to some church or other.

The Romans think they have a monopoly on salvation and dispense it only to those who are Roman Catholic Christians who keep the R.C. rules. They claim You granted them the exclusive franchise for salvation and personally drew up the rules, which is something I think You ought to be pretty sore about. I mean, if You are God, You can't actually be that narrow-minded, and I don't think You ought to let anyone get away with claiming that You are. It gives You a bad name among people who do their own thinking.

Some other branches of Your supposed church want to make assent to certain creedal statements the test of salvation, which is also pretty silly, especially when you know how orthodox creeds such as the one formulated at Nicaea got to be approved as orthodox.

Other branches of the church make their pitch on the basis of an emotional experience, conversion, giving your heart to Christ, that sort of thing. They claim that this emotional experience will transform, say, a mean, sensual, weak, or evil character into a fine, decent, pleasant, ascetic character.

I just don't believe it. A "conversion experience" usually causes the converted to exercise his meanness or sensuality or whatever according to a new set of values, true. A drunk can become the most aggressive member of the temperance society. A sensualist can turn from chasing women to chasing the sellers of girlie magazines. A mean unrighteous man can be easily converted into a mean righteous man. This happens all the time. In that sense, conversion can, and often does, make a man a more acceptable citizen. But this isn't a cure

CHARLES MERRILL SMITH

64

of souls. It is more like a cure of antisocial tendencies, which isn't the same thing at all.

The trouble is, Sir, a genuine cure of souls is a long and difficult business. If I read the New Testament correctly, "salvation" means "health of spirit, wholeness of soul." And if I understand the biblical doctrine of creation, it says that body and soul are just our way of describing something that is all of a piece, that body and soul cannot be divided.

If this is the case, then salvation has to do with the whole person—his body, his spirit, his environment, his needs as a human being, his aspirations, his frustrations, all of him. That's why I think the techniques of salvation practiced by the various branches of Christendom are too cheap and easy. You can't deal with the whole person by handing him a set of rules to keep, or saying "sign this creed," or getting him to make "a decision for Christ."

If the new church, which we all hope will emerge in the near future, is to practice a genuine cure of souls, it will have to give up on these old, easy approaches to salvation.

This means, or at least I think it means, that the church will need the barest minimum of institution, no more than one-tenth, if that much, of the plant it now has and the operation of which occupies so much of the clergyman's time and energy. It will need practically none of the programs which the churches are currently pushing. It may even mean abandoning the idea of a paid professional clergy and expecting all the members to be ministers. (I have a theory that once a church has paid executives with expense accounts it has become institutionalized beyond hope of reformation, but I could be a little too radical about this, I suppose.)

Right now, most of the churches are floundering around trying to figure out what they ought to be doing, and the professional clergyman is wondering if his profession is obsolete. (I expect You have been receiving quite a few prayers lately from troubled members of the clergy.) But in a church organized to cure souls the church would have something to do which needs doing, and the clergyman—whether paid or volunteer—would find a significant role.

I don't know how You feel about it, Sir, but I believe the day is done when the preacher can tell secular society how to behave because "this is the Christian way." Too many preachers who don't know what they are talking about have laid down Christian prescriptions for the improvement of society. These prescriptions have been, usually, oversimple solutions to complex problems based on ignorance or at least inadequate social, political, and psychological information.

Now don't get me wrong. I don't mean that the preacher shouldn't be a prophet. I don't want any part of that brand of Christianity which says, "Let the preacher deal with the spiritual side of man and keep his hands off the secular side of his life." Neither Amos nor Jesus would have taken kindly to such a suggestion. Besides which, every crook, charlatan, exploiter, every greedy operator, racist, Fascist, Communist—everyone who is up to no good—holds that view. But instead of pushing reform schemes and political solutions (which most preachers aren't equipped to evaluate), let the leadership of the new church proclaim the conditions of life which are essential to a healthy spirit. In this area a Christian ought to be able to speak with some authority.

Are adequate food, housing, clothing, and health care necessary if one is to have a healthy spirit? Maybe not absolutely necessary. The human spirit can survive, apparently, up against great privation. But they help a lot. Jesus admonished his disciples to see to these things—feed the hungry, clothe the naked. (We ought to understand that a few Christmas baskets to the deserving poor and sending our old blue serge suits to the natives of south sea islands isn't exactly what Jesus had in mind.) Anyway, we Christians believe that Jesus spoke by Your authority, and that's pretty good authority.

And Jesus, according to the New Testament, spent much of his time healing spiritual ills. Is that not Your mandate to the church to go and do likewise?

As I look back on thirty years in the parish, I now see that the things I thought were most important when I was doing them really weren't very important.

I built buildings, raised money in the millions to pay off building indebtedness and to keep the plant running, preached what I thought were incisive, literarily respectable sermons. Oh yes, I also spent plenty of time counseling with troubled people, trying to comfort the bereaved, helping untangle human messes of one kind and another, teaching, being there when someone needed me. But I believed at the time that the people side of the profession was incidental to the institutional side. After all, the bishop never knew about the people I helped over the hump of some personal difficulty or tragedy. I didn't get any institutional points for teaching children. Time spent working with a family in trouble was time stolen from my administrative duties.

Now I believe that about the only monuments I left behind are the people I helped. A lot of them needed more help than I was qualified to give them it is true. Often they needed a psychiatrist or clinical psychologist or a trained family counselor or a lawyer or a social worker. I did the best I could because so seldom was there anyone around to refer them to.

If I had it to do over, I would insist that the church forego erecting that beautiful, fancy building which cost so much to build and maintain, and put the money into people help. And as our society becomes more complex, impersonal, bureaucratized, and computerized, the need for people to have some place to go where someone will deal with them as people will grow enormously. If the church would program itself to be that kind of place, then maybe the world would pay some attention to it, and maybe the clergyman wouldn't be obsolete.

A social club with a slightly pious flavor, who needs it? But a place where souls are cured, there is a need for that. So please try, Sir, to get that message across when You send down Your revelation on what the church of Jesus Christ should be in the modern world.

CHARLES MERRILL SMITH

12

Do You Expect Us to Be Perfect?

Flawless Sir . . . I once knew a lady who had a splendid Christian character, was much given to good works, passionately devoted to the cause of Christian missions, tireless in her service to the church, and a supporter of every worthwhile community project. I suppose it is a commentary on the image of the upright Christian personality that this description makes her sound pretty forbidding as a person. But she wasn't. She was a pleasant, likeable lady—I was about to say "in spite of her goodness," but that wouldn't be nice.

Anyway, I discovered by accident that she was a secret but enthusiastic player of the ponies. She had something down on the fifth at Aqueduct or the daily double at Arlington Park almost every day the horses were running.

Talk about the incongruous! Here was this very model of the Christian personality who eschewed every appearance of evil but liked to bet on the horses. Her church had specific injunctions against gambling. Some of the money she gave (and generously) to her church was used to lobby against legalized gambling.

Now here's the kicker. After I found out about her secret sin (using sin in the popular rather than the theological meaning of the term), I liked her better. This crack in the façade of her Christian perfection made her more appealing as a person.

Oh, I know a two-dollar bet on the bangtails isn't a mortal sin, and it isn't even a very serious venial sin. That's not the point. The point is, why did I like her better after I discovered that she was a flawed Christian vessel?

Maybe it was because, knowing my own shortcomings, it made me feel better to discover that she was imperfect too. It is no secret that most of us feel better about our own imperfections if the sterling characters we know turn out to be not so good as everyone supposes. That is a pretty chintzy way to improve one's moral estimate of himself, but most of us do it.

Everyone, of course, is delighted when someone who pretends to be better than everyone else takes a moral tumble. When the upright banker absconds with the cash balance or the righteous Sunday school teacher is apprehended *in flagrante delicto* with a lady of the evening, we all say, "How shocking!" but what we mean is, "How pleasing and satisfying to me this is!" It's a despicable reaction, of course, on our part—but quite common.

CHARLES MERRILL SMITH

But this isn't the kind of a reaction I'm talking about in the case of the Christian horseplayer. I'm puzzled by the discrepancy between the Christian perfection of character we all are supposed to be striving for, and the way I'm put off by the people who, to the eye of the observer, have attained it. Theoretically I should have found that the fact the lady was a secret gambler lowered her in my estimation, but what it did was to raise her in my estimation.

Could it be that we are striving for the wrong thing when we lay down our churchly rules for ideal Christian character? Is a sort of sterile goodness what You really expect of us? Why is it that, when it comes to people, absolute perfection puts us off a little?

Does it put You off a little too?

13

The Joys and Dolors of Middle Age

Rock of Ages, Sir . . . As I mentioned in an earlier talk, I am now in the prime of life, which is a euphemism for middle age. Our current youth culture considers my generation hopelessly ancient and would no doubt consign us to the mercies of the gas chamber were euthanasia lawful.

Actually, I haven't found being middle aged all that bad. It takes more pills, panaceas, ungents, and doctor's bills to keep me going than were necessary a decade ago, naturally. I have lost whatever youthful allure I ever had. But the kids are raised. I can live quite comfortably on much less money than I thought possible when I was forty. I no longer need suffer from the young man's disease of trying to prove himself. These are all big plusses to my way of thinking, even taking into account the extra upkeep on my physical machinery.

But Sir, I haven't adjusted completely yet. Maybe my case is unique, though I doubt it. Maybe it's just the male menopause, if there is such a thing. But I found, as I approached fifty, that my world of values began to crumble. That, Sir, is no fun for anyone.

For example, all my life I had believed that our social institutions were beneficent in intent though sometimes bumbling in performance. Now I wonder if any institutions—political, educational, religious—are interested in anything but their own preservation.

I hate feeling this way. I hate it because, on the one hand is my conviction that social stability and the passing on of what's best in human thought and culture depends on institutions. On the other hand, though, is the dismaying knowledge that these institutions, today, are doing a rotten job of it and show little inclination to do better. I have this frightful feeling that all my beloved institutions are going to try to save too much out of the past and end up losing everything.

Take another example, Sir. I have always operated on the principle that what You really wanted was people who were good, more or less open-minded, reasonably liberal, and that our society would be best for everybody when it came to be run along the lines and according to the values of the United Methodist Church. (This is a belief, I might add, shared by most standard brand Protestants and practically all Methodists.) Now I no longer consider any of this desirable. It may have been a silly set of values, but even silly values, long cherished, are not given up without anguish.

I would guess that not a few people in my age bracket are

going through the same spiritual upheaval. One way to deal with the trauma is, the more uncertain you become of what you hold to be good and true, the more rigid you are in defending your shaky convictions. It's like the guy who is constantly telling you what a great marriage he has—pretty soon you begin to wonder who he's trying to convince. Passionate advocates of old orthodoxies of any kind often strike me as scared, spiritually disturbed people who see their value systems collapsing.

The other response, or adjustment mechanism, is the one I use, which is to reexamine my values. I don't claim it is any better than the rigid defense mechanism, but I think it is—in the beginning anyway—more painful to the soul.

It seems to me, Sir, that a man of middle years ought to be secure in his values and convictions. He's had half a century to put together a working knowledge of what life is all about based on observation and experience. I have always believed that age is accompanied by wisdom, but it hasn't worked out that way for me. When I was thirty-five, I had all the answers. Now I'm not even sure as to what are the questions.

It could be that I'm too dumb to catch on, or so *non compos mentis* that I learn nothing from experience, but naturally I reject these suppositions. I have a theory, much more flattering to me than that I'm stupid, but still reasonable I think, that what a Christian is going through today must be very much like what Christians went through during the Protestant Reformation. You would know better than I do what that was like, of course, but the Reformation must have done strange things to people.

A fifty-year-old man living in Switzerland, say, where some

of the cantons stuck by Rome and others opted for Luther's movement, could have become an emotional basket case rather easily. All his life he had never questioned the validity of the Roman church and its world-view, then all of a sudden large chunks of the world were rejecting papal authority, the monolithic claims of the Vatican, etc. In other words, the world was shattering his value system before his eyes. A serious, sensitive man, such as I fancy I am, can't go through that without some spiritual torment.

Maybe I should be cheered by the subsequent history of the Reformation. As You know, it wasn't all good, but apparently it was a necessary corrective to old, tired, erroneous ideas and systems. And the world rolled right on; people somehow adjusted to the new order of things.

What I am saying, Sir, is that I wish I had that peace of mind and spirit which comes only to people who have no doubts or questions about their values. I have always been taught that Christians, if they are the real article, always have this inner peace. It's supposed to be a sort of reward from You for having unquestioning faith.

Well, I don't have it, and if that makes me a bum Christian then I'm a bum Christian. I have an exuberance in living, a great sense of joy in Your creation. But I still have this spiritual malaise whenever (and it's frequent) I inventory my values.

I hope You won't hold it against me, and I really don't think that You will. That's one value I'm pretty sure of.

HOW TO TALK TO GOD . . .

14

What Do You Think of Madalyn Murray O'Hair?

Great Judge of Us All, Sir . . . Did You catch the "Phil Donahue Show" the other day (it's a syndicated TV show) when he had the Reverend Bob Harrington and Madalyn Murray O'Hair on it? No doubt You know them both quite well. Bob Harrington is the famous chaplain of Bourbon Street in New Orleans (not a very godly street, I'm afraid), and Madalyn Murray O'Hair is the famous atheist who claims You don't exist.

In case You missed it, let me say that it was a pretty good show, or at least I thought so.

Chaplain Bob is a big, beefy, jubilant Christian who candidly admits that, with the help of Jesus, he has licked all the sins of the flesh except gluttony. His theology strikes me as appalling, but he's rather appealing. He spouts a narrow, simplistic, pious-cliché-ridden brand of Christianity, but he has none of the thin-lipped, malicious-spirited, prideful qualities which so often characterize this type of Christian. I'm convinced that he really loves those sinners he works with, and that makes up for a lot of bad theology.

Suprisingly, Madalyn is also a jovial soul. If Chaplain Bob is on the theological right, then she is somewhere way up in the left-field bleachers. Her theology, if an avowed atheist's beliefs can be called theology, is about as intellectually acceptable as Chaplain Bob's, which is to say that hers isn't very good either. For example, if I heard her correctly, she claimed Jesus never existed, which is prejudiced nonsense that would shock any knowledgeable atheist.

Anyway, they had a lively dialogue. I expected they would tear each other to shreds, but they didn't. They argued heatedly, sure, but without any of the bitterness or rancor which is so often present in theological debates, even among Christian theologians who are all supposed to be on Your side. I got the impression that they liked each other quite well.

I wonder what You think of Madalyn O'Hair? She's been going around knocking You for years. I've been taught that, sooner or later, You always zap people like that. But I'd like to put in a plea for You to withhold judgment on her until You review her case.

In the first place, she's not going to do You any real harm. She isn't going to corrupt anyone that isn't already corrupted.

Secondly, she is, I believe, a basically happy, life-accepting person who is grateful (not to You, of course) for the privilege of enjoying this good world. That ought to earn her some heavenly Brownie points because too many Christians are a long way behind her in this.

Thirdly, I think she is absolutely honest. Does that count for something in celestial scorekeeping?

One thing about Mrs. O'Hair does disturb me. She is apparently the equal of Chaplain Bob as far as being a happy, joyful person is concerned. Christians are supposed to believe that Christians alone are completely happy and joyful, but Mrs. O'Hair, I believe, can hold her own with most Christians in the happiness department.

Why is this, Sir? Is it because some people are just happy by nature? If so, that invalidates one of the best reasons for becoming a Christian. Or is it because atheists can be just as happy as Christians but they don't know why they are happy, and Christians do? Perhaps we ought to discuss this further.

If You didn't tune in on the show maybe You'd be interested in my evaluation of who won the debate. I'd say that Madalyn had a little the best of it because she has mastered the trick of keeping her opponent on the defensive, but actually it was pretty much of a draw.

CHARLES MERRILL SMITH

78

15

Should Pat Boone Have Been Excommunicated?

Source of All Wisdom, Sir . . . I'd like Your opinion on a news item I came across today. Seems that Pat Boone (You know, the big singing, movie, TV star) and his wife have been excommunicated (he called it "disfellowshiped") from a denomination known as the Churches of Christ (not to be confused with the Disciples of Christ or the United Church of Christ—these denominational labels do become confusing).

Now we know that the Churches of Christ are a fundamentalist group with rather strict rules of conduct, so one might think that Pat had been catting around or overindulging in the lures of this present world, characteristics not uncommon to the show business milieu. Given the C of C's outlook on personal behavior I could have understood it if something along this line had been the reason for Pat's disenfranchisement.

But that wasn't it. He got the old ecclesiastical boot because he and his wife have been practicing faith healing and glossalalia. (I'm sure You read Greek, so I don't have to explain that glossalalia isn't something dirty, but only the practice of speaking in tongues.) He also has been baptizing people in his swimming pool (heated), but that wasn't cited as a reason for dismissal.

Well now, Sir, I don't want to get into the merits of faith healing or ecstatic utterances. That sort of thing isn't my bag. But who can deny that the New Testament speaks approvingly of both practices (although, as You will remember, St. Paul cautioned moderation and care in the use of tongues)? What gets me is that the Churches of Christ insist that the only certified Christian is one who believes the Bible as literally interpreted, then when Pat and his wife practice the New Testament literally they get canned out of the church. These people, it seems to me, must have holes in their heads to kick out of the church someone who has only followed to its logical limits the fundamental teaching of that church. How does it seem to You?

In one sense I have a sneaking admiration for the Churches of Christ, though. However illogical its reasons, it does take courage to give the heave-ho to the denomination's most famous layman and probably one of its biggest contributors.

Any denomination loves to bag a film star or professional sports hero because such people are the idols of our culture. I mean, if they can, by their endorsement, persuade people to buy a certain brand of beer or underarm deodorant, they can sell a certain brand of religion too. Pat says that since the

CHARLES MERRILL SMITH

80

word has gotten around that he is out of the C of C, several denominations, including the Mormons, who may go in for faith healing and glossalalia for all I know, and the Methodists, who don't, have been hot on his trail. I'll bet if it had been Joe Glotz who got kicked out, the Mormons and the Methodists wouldn't be burning a path to his door.

Just so You won't think I'm prejudiced against the fundamentalists, I also know a big fancy liberal church which preaches that Christians shouldn't drink, but it also balances its budget with the income from the bar of a hotel which it owns.

So if I sound a bit cynical about such inconsistencies and insanities practiced in the name of Christ, it is because I am. Cynicism isn't a very nice attitude, but I'm not going to apologize for it. In such cases it is the only appropriate response I can think of.

16

My Wife Says I'm a Square

Creative Spirit, Sir . . . My wife says I'm a square. It isn't that she wants me to wear bell-bottoms, don love beads, learn to play the guitar, or incorporate other facets of the hippie culture into my life-style. In the argot of the day "square" also means any person who is limited in imagination and slow to accept new modes of thinking. That's what she says I am.

I know You are supposed to be everywhere and can tune in on anybody's private life even better than J. Edgar Hoover, so presumably You could know what our argument (friendly) is all about. Somehow, though, I conceive You as too much of a gentleman to be a celestial voyeur, so I had better tell You about it.

You see, my wife is hung up on Edgar Cayce, ESP, the

occult. This is very much "in" today, especially among kids, so by that standard she is with it. Since I am highly skeptical about all this stuff, I'm out of it.

My problem, she thinks, is that I overdepend on the rational and short-change the superrational or the extrarational. In other words, I'm suspicious of any claim which cannot be supported by well-documented evidence and fitted into a logical pattern. What I need to know is, is this bad?

Oh, I can buy extrasensory perception. It is somewhat spooky, I admit, but there is enough evidence to lend it credibility. It's the foretelling of the future through visions, dreams, etc., the ghosts who hang around a house for centuries raising merry hell with the living, the communications from "the other side" which I can't swallow.

Take the case of Jeane Dixon, a lady who claims to be on excellent terms with You. She insists she has these visions which inform her as to when the next war will occur (next big, mind-blowing war, that is), and when a president is going to be assassinated, and who will be elected. She implies that because she is a virtuous, orthodox Christian lady You reward her by sending her these visions. It's like she has a direct TV hookup to heaven and she is the only one on the cable.

Well, I may be ill informed in the ways of clairvoyants, but I do know enough theology to state flatly that she is full of theological prunes if she thinks that's why she gets these future news flashes. Analyze her claim and she is saying, in effect, that God can be bribed just like a politician or tax assessor. I'll defend You against such a calumny with my last breath. Even supposing she is tapped into a divine pipeline there has got to be a better reason.

HOW TO TALK TO GOD . . .

I like Edgar Cayce's approach better. He said he didn't have a clue as to why he could diagnose diseases that doctors couldn't, or how all this information came to him in a trance. He didn't make any financial killing out of his gift or whatever it was like Jeane Dixon has. He was suspicious of his own powers and handled them gingerly. I tend to take seriously the claims of a seer who refuses to exploit his odd ability. People who use the power to rake it in are bound to be self-serving in their claims and almost bound to puff their successes and conceal their failures.

But to get back to the point, I need a lot of convincing before I accept any of this. Someone could say, "Well, you believe in God, and that's a matter of faith rather than evidence," and I wouldn't have much of a comeback, would I?

Or would I? In the first place, I can see a reasonable pattern leading me to believe in Your existence. Of course, I don't know for certain what You are like. But the Bible and the theologians say You are the creator, and that makes sense to me. Oh, I know some scientists claim that the hypothesis of a creator is not necessary to explain the existence of the universe. And I confess I am out of my depth here. But I once asked an atomic physicist who is an exponent of the Big Bang theory of creation what was behind the big bang. He replied that science could only get back to the cosmic explosion, but not behind it. So until science tells me something else is behind the bang I'll stick with my conviction that You did it.

Also, if human life has any meaning or purpose—and while the existentialists and others will argue that it doesn't, it seems to me on the basis of the evidence that it does— then it appeals to me as reasonable that this meaning and

CHARLES MERRILL SMITH

purpose derive from a creator who knew what He had in mind. I could go on, but You grasp what I am getting at, I'm sure.

Now none of this is hard evidence in the scientific sense. Ultimately I have to believe in You by faith. But it is faith founded on a pattern, a reasonable proposition.

A reasonable pattern is what I find lacking in the claims of the occult. Maybe there is some reason why heavenly visions should be vouchsafed to Jeane Dixon instead of Brigitte Bardot, but I can't discover it. Perhaps there are ghosts all over the place, but what purpose do they serve? Perhaps I ought to believe in all the spooky stuff so popular today, but why?

You know, Sir, the disciple I identify with isn't the Big Fisherman, much as I admire him, or John, reputedly Jesus' favorite, nice guy that he must have been. The one I identify with is Thomas. Preachers have given Thomas a hard time of it over the centuries, calling him "Doubting Thomas" and other bad names. But when the disciples were standing around the risen Christ, he was the only one who said, "O.K., let's look at the evidence."

I expect that's what I would have done had I been one of the group. So I'm awfully glad that the New Testament doesn't say anything bad about Thomas. It's a comfort to me.

17

Do You Want Us to Love the Communists?

All-Loving Sir . . . Now that our U.S. Ping-Pong team has breached the great wall of Red China, a phenomenon unthinkable a few years ago, should we American Christians soften up our attitude toward communism in general?

The way it is now, if you are heard to express anything but a hostile attitude toward communism, you risk community censure, the John Birch Society will be on your neck, and the FBI may be bugging your phone.

We American Christians, while believing that You love everyone, wonder how You can actually love Communists. I was in this group of Christian laymen, and they got to discussing the late Bishop James Pike. They didn't like him very well, and finally one fellow said, "He was a Commie, wasn't he?" I suppose Jim Pike is with You now, so You could check it out with him, but I never saw a particle of evidence that he ever had the slightest sympathy for communism. So I told this joker who said he was a Commie that that was just a lot of baloney. (I didn't exactly say "baloney." I hope you will forgive me.)

The point is that we have been conditioned to think that when anyone wants to say the worst thing possible about someone the thing to do is to call him a Commie. Are we going to change all that, and if so, is it good or bad?

I'm not very hot for communism myself. Once I was behind the iron curtain and it was a creepy experience, rather like the ambience of a grade B Nazi movie. Everyone looked like they felt like I feel when I go for a tax audit. I wouldn't want to live in such a place.

Also, communism as a philosophy is founded on a gross misconception of human nature, or so I think. But then it is to my advantage to preserve things as they are. What stake I have in life is in what we loosely refer to as the "establishment," and, come the revolution, I'll probably be liquidated. Is this a good enough reason for me to hate communism?

Personally I don't think the Reds have a prayer of taking over the United States. A Fascist movement backed by the military, that might happen here, but not a Communist uprising. The Commies can't even breathe life into their moribund American party.

But they might surround us with Communist countries. South America could become one big Cuba. Then what do we do?

I have this haunting suspicion that, as much as I dislike

HOW TO TALK TO GOD . . .

communism, if I were some poor slob in the hellish slums of Lima, I'd be one. I was in Cuba (on an evangelistic mission, as I hope You will recall) shortly before Castro took over. I lived with the poor people for a short time. Believe me, I would have backed Castro. He may be pretty bad, but nothing could have been worse than what he replaced.

So what is the Christian attitude toward communism? Can I thoroughly dislike the system but love the people? Do You prefer one political system over another?

I expect that there's going to be a lot of Christian flak over the proper attitude toward Commies now that we are making China respectable again. We really could use some divine guidance on this.

CHARLES MERRILL SMITH

18

What Should We Christians Be Doing about Pornography?

All-Enlightened Sir . . . Do You have showings of the latest films in the Great Hall of Heaven like they do at the White House? Aren't those skin flicks something else! Even the regular product of Hollywood shows one more these days than we used to get in the stag movies at the American Legion smoker. And if You ever stroll along 42nd Street between Broadway and 8th Avenue, catch the covers on the porno magazines on display in about every other store window. My! My!

My question is, should Christians be doing something to rid the theaters and newsstands of dirty, sexually oriented films and publications? There is much agitation for stricter censorship, and many of the agitators are Christians who are agitating out of Christian conviction.

Believe me, Sir, I've done a powerful amount of soul searching and spiritual handwringing over the problem of Christian censorship. Here are some of my conclusions.

1. Smutty stuff, filmed or printed, which conveys the concept that sex is dirty, grotesque, or impersonal has to be judged as contrary to the Christian belief that sex is fundamentally good and beautiful. If You are in touch with the situation You know that a great deal of porno material is pretty kinky.

2. Although sex-oriented material is the prime target of the censorship crusade, there is a growing revulsion at the mindless violence portrayed in sadomasochistic contexts in the junk films and magazines, but also in family movies and TV. Christians, as a rule, are more appalled by the sexual trash. That is only to be expected because, in our culture, sex is considered more disreputable than violence. But violence is beginning to turn us off, too.

3. While there appears to be no solid evidence that pornography generates antisocial behavior, I can't help but believe that the portrayal of sex as a coarse animal function and violence as a mark of manhood must produce some pretty unhealthy attitudes in those exposed to it. Therefore, from the Christian point of view, which values love, gentleness, and responsible treatment of our fellow-man, it would be better if we didn't have pornography.

4. I can see no way of suppressing this objectionable material without giving up the right to freedom of expression so cherished by and basic to our American way of life.

Do You perceive my dilemma?

As a Christian I find pornography objectionable and would

CHARLES MERRILL SMITH

like to see it done away with. As an American who is committed to upholding freedom of expression, I see no way to eliminate pornography apart from sacrificing this freedom. I don't like either option. I assume You dislike pornography as much as I do, because if I believe the witness of the Scriptures it is a distortion of what You intend us to be as human beings. But the suppression of our freedom to express ourselves also distorts us as human beings. How would You choose between these unappetizing alternatives?

Let me submit my present thinking on the subject and see what You think of it.

My conclusions are based on the history of Christian censorship. As You know, Christians and the Christian Church have always been among the first to nominate themselves for the office of censor. Today, in countries such as Spain, or even more enlightened societies such as Ireland, where the church has a dominant position and a close relationship with the government, the church decides what people can or can't read, hear, or see.

From the church's performance one has to conclude, Sir, that communications between You and it have broken down. These are usually Roman Catholic countries, but there is no evidence that a dominant Protestantism would be any better. From personal experience with them I have found that the Protestant Christians who want to be censors consider *Rebecca of Sunnybrook Farm* a bit racy, and anything but the more innocuous of Walt Disney's films unacceptable.

Suprisingly, these extreme Protestants aren't bothered much by violence. Recently I heard Dale Evans, the movies' famed cowgirl and purportedly a devout Protestant Christian, condemn the current sexy trend in movies. Then she went ahead to say her idea of a wholesome movie was the latest John Wayne epic which fairly drips gore and is full of gun fights and people beating up on other people.

Governments, of course—even ours—favor the principle of censorship. They aren't much interested in the morals of books and movies, but if it is established that literary and esthetic values are censorable, then it follows that political expression can also be regulated. Politicians and government bureaucrats find the charms of political censorship irresistible.

So, for me, the whole dilemma spins around the question of who is to be the censor.

In almost every community in which I have ever lived some Christian group has attempted to enlist me in a campaign to clean up the newsstands or dictate to the theater owner. Up to now I have an unsmirched record of refusing to be a part of such a campaign, and I intend to preserve it unsmirched for as long as I can keep my wits about me. Perhaps as my brain softens and I decline into senility I may change my position, but until that unhappy day no one need count on me to be a censor.

It isn't that I feel unqualified for the job. I believe myself to be the only completely reliable censor of books, movies, TV, etc. I know. But I won't last forever, and then who could we get to fill the job?

That, of course, is exactly what's wrong with Christian censorship. Everybody feels as I do about themselves. They know what is good for people and what is bad for people. The only difference is that many Christians are willing to impose their taste and judgment on others, and I am not.

CHARLES MERRILL SMITH

Censorship is like calculating the exact Christian length for ladies' skirts. I have some ideas on the subject, but I would not want to be arbitrary about it.

These are the reasons why, forced to select one or the other options, I vote against censorship. It is choosing between catastrophes, I know, but suppression of free speech I believe to be the greater disaster.

Am I wrong about this?

19

What Do I Do about Those Little Guilt Feelings?

Divine Forgiver, Sir . . . I see by the papers that Lieutenant Calley, presumably engulfed with delayed remorse over his mindless slaughter of defenseless civilians, is turning to You seeking forgiveness. No one doubts that You will grant him absolution, for You can't be You and refuse. Also, I'll bet that the lieutenant won't ever harm a fly again. He's had it with sinning, at least on the grand scale.

My complaint, for it is in the nature of a complaint, is that the spectacular sinner would seem to have a spiritual advantage over us pedestrian transgressors. A monstrous guilt receives a king-size forgiveness, which more often than not issues in a redeemed personality. Lieutenant Calley, I'll wager, will go and sin no more.

But what about me? If I were a Roman Catholic and went to

confession, I'd bore my confessor with the triviality of my sins.

Do you recall the story about Martin Luther who, in his pre-Reformation days, was such a compulsive confessor of moral peccadilloes that his priest, in exasperation, told him to commit some interesting sins in order to relieve the tedium of the confessions?

That's the way I feel about my sins. Like most respectable middle-class Christians I am either too chicken to transgress on a dramatic scale or lack the imagination to be an interesting sinner.

I doubt that You would care to hear about my sins. I'm not always good-tempered and sweet-spirited. I spend too large a proportion of my income on myself and don't share enough of it with others. I don't suffer fools and bores gladly. I enjoy imposing my will on other people, but resent it when other people try to impose their will on me. I permit myself to hurt from anxieties and depressions, which are really only a form of overweening self-concern, and You know what Jesus said about excessive self-concern.

Now none of these sins would cause anyone to ooh! and ah! as they do when hearing accounts of lurid and juicy trespasses. You may be yawning over them. But I still feel guilty.

Part of the problem, no doubt, is that Lieutenant Calley, bathed in the miracle of divine pardon for his revolting act, knows that he is a new man and won't ever do that again. But even if you forgive, say, my uneven temperament or petty selfishness, I doubt that I'll improve much.

HOW TO TALK TO GOD . .

Is divine forgiveness, then, commensurate with the size of the transgression? Does a big sin receive a giant cup of pardon, while a minuscule offense gets only a demitasse? Theologically this is an absurd idea, but—for me, at least—it seems psychologically consistent.

I want to talk some more about guilt in our next conversation, for after all it is one of the main concerns of the Christian. But meanwhile, I need some reassurance.

Do You listen to the confession of my boring sins as attentively as You hear the technicolor accounts from fascinating sinners and their mind-boggling moral irregularities? If so, is Your forgiveness for me as generous as it is for them?

I expect that You do and it is. I need to believe this.

CHARLES MERRILL SMITH

20

Is All This Guilt Really Necessary?

Understanding Spirit, Sir . . . To continue our conversation about guilt, sometimes I wonder if You expect us to feel as guilty about as many things as we are taught that You do.

Any carefully raised Christian, which I am, whether he be Catholic or Protestant, has a well-developed case of the guilts from before puberty on.

Sex is our big hang-up, as I have mentioned to You previously. It ranges from the really weird stuff they pound into young Catholic seminarians about how to avoid touching their "privates" and how to conjure up disgusting images of females when being assaulted by sexual temptation, to the common preachments that sex is disgusting to You except when performed within wedlock.

Leaving aside the pros and cons of that argument, the upshot has been that people who have had it dinned into them that sex is basically sinful except within prescribed limits carry over this sinful feeling about it even within the sanctioned limits. In other words, guilt can't be turned on and off like the lavatory tap.

But Christian guilt feelings aren't limited to sex. There is this moral pressure to be a success as success is defined by society (a pressure directly traceable to the Protestant Ethic). I know people who have lived miserable lives because they couldn't measure up, not to mention a few who blew their brains out because they couldn't live with the guilt of failure. They believed that You didn't like them, because if You liked them You would have seen to it that they prospered.

We are taught to feel guilty, we Christians, when we transgress the mores, the cultural prescriptions of our society. I recall the juvenile terror which descended on me the first time I went to a movie on Sunday. That seems pretty quaint now, but the terror was real. After all, my conservative Protestant subculture assured me that going to the movies on Sunday was one of the things You hated most, and that You might knock me around severely for such an infraction of divine law. (I expected to get it that very night, or at least the next morning, and was very surprised when, apparently, You weren't troubled about it at all.)

Well, Sir, don't laugh. Silly as it sounds, this is an excellent example of the guilt business as practiced in Your name by Your people. It's as if the Christian leadership has no confidence in the pulling power of heaven, but is pretty sure everyone wants to escape going to hell.

The trouble is, guilt is habit forming. I have long since

CHARLES MERRILL SMITH

98

dissociated myself intellectually from the standard Christian guilt syndrome, but I can't break the habit entirely.

For example, one of the moral tests of any proposed action we were taught to give ourselves was, "Would you want to be doing this when Jesus comes?" That is an outrageous, stupid, irrelevant test if I ever heard one. If one followed it literally, he would be afraid to go to the bathroom. No one but a spiritual sadist would recommend it, and only a retarded member of the Jukes family would take it seriously.

But, Sir, do You know that I still catch myself asking this question of myself, and sometimes feel an initial flash of spiritual anxiety when contemplating the most harmless of pastimes?

Please do not leap to the conclusion that I want to eliminate all guilt. There is legitimate guilt. Some guilt feelings are well earned, and these should produce the moral d.t.'s.

But there has been so much phony guilt visited upon us by grotesque and usually superficial concepts of sin that a moratorium on guilt-exploiting religion would, it seems to me, be a blessing. If the Christian church can't keep going except on guilt power, then I say let it die and good riddance. We can always start a new one founded on a surer rock.

I know I sound rather hostile about this. It is only because I feel rather hostile about it. I ought to feel guilty about my hostile feelings, I know, and sooner or later I suppose I shall.

But not now.

21

How Do I Handle My Hostilities?

Ever-Patient Sir . . . I ended our last conversation by admitting I was hostile toward something and commenting that, sooner or later, I would feel guilty about my hostility.

Well, I'm feeling guilty now. I feel guilty because hostility feelings are antithetical to the Christian belief that the spirit of love is the appropriate human attitude toward people and the world. Besides, hostile feelings push up my blood pressure, which is too high already.

But how do I curb my hostilities?

It's no good telling me to be sweet, patient, and long-suffering. I am not, by nature, sweet, patient, and long-suffering. And so often the world conspires against my best efforts to cool it and suppress my hostilities.

Take an example. The other day I had occasion to deal with a government agency, a bureaucracy. Now if there is anything calculated to blow the mind of even the calmest of men it is dealing with a bureaucracy.

In the first place, I always approach authority of any kind with trepidation. A bureaucracy may be staffed with idiots, incompetents, and surly boobs, but it has the power to complicate my life. If I am treated discourteously, as so often is the case, I can't fight back because I need that license or receipt or whatever, and the cretin behind the desk can always find a rule for delaying or denying what I need. He can foul things up for me if my haircut offends him, or if he has indigestion, or for no discernible reason. My experience with bureaucracies isn't always bad, but it is bad enough of the time that I am hostile towards all bureaucracies all of the time.

I always pump up plenty of hostility toward people who I suspect do not regard me as highly as I think they ought. I feel like blowing a gasket when someone frustrates my plans and projects. I am hostile toward Melvin Laird. No rational reason for it. When I see him on the tube, I feel the irritability rising like the thermometer in a heat wave.

I notice that the Gospels record some instances in which Jesus expressed attitudes—towards the Pharisees, for instance—that could be construed as hostility. Is there a clue here for me? Is there a legitimate hostility and an illegitimate hostility? What determines the difference?

However, I don't want to pass off my hostility as righteous indignation. Some of it may be that, but I certainly wouldn't try to kid You, Sir, that all or any major portion of it is righteous. Personally, I don't like hostile people. They turn me off. So what I dislike in others and call bad I refuse to permit in myself and call it good.

But I haven't learned how to quell my hostile feelings yet. Maybe I'm just an irascible type, but that is a mealy-mouthed excuse and probably not acceptable in heaven.

So do You have any suggestions for handling this problem?

CHARLES MERRILL SMITH

22

Were All These Colors Really Necessary?

All-Wise Sir . . . One shouldn't question the wisdom of Divinity, but I can't help but wonder sometimes if You wouldn't have been smarter to have made us all one color. Of course a monochrome humanity would make for a drab scene, which is why, I suppose, You chose to create the rich variety of brown people and black people and yellow people and red people, and pinkish-grey people (which we call white), and maybe on other planets purple people and polka-dot people. But Sir, have You contemplated the messy human relationships caused by all these colors?

Let me make it clear before You give me a black mark for spiritual pride, which I know from reading the Bible is the worst of all sins, that while I believe with my mind that color doesn't make any difference, I have emotions which cause me to react as if it does.

103

Perhaps up there in heaven You are so far removed from the daily grind on earth that the Celestial Council or whatever You call Your cabinet or advisors has failed to call Your attention to this problem as frequently as it should. Believe me, Sir, we have odd and irrational ways of thinking and acting about the color problem down here. Of course, You know everything, so there is no need to enlighten You. However, it occurred to me that Gabriel and Moses and St. Paul, all of whom are no doubt valued counselors, along with others of Your official family, perhaps need to have the situation down here clarified for them. Therefore, I have prepared another fable which I hope will aid them in understanding how we handle the color problem, as well as afford them a bit of entertainment. I call it

THE LEOPARDS WITHOUT ANY SPOTS

Once in Africa, or maybe it was India, there was a colony of albino leopards. Nobody knew why these leopards were white in color and had no spots whatever, but it didn't seem to be any handicap to them to be white and spotless, so the tribe prospered. It developed its own leopard culture. The tribe spoke leopard language of course, but with a distinctive accent, not too dissimilar from South Carolina Geechtee or Mississippi Delta. The albino leopards were strong and speedy and especially adept at hunting. But, living in isolation, they were unsophisticated and not wise to the ways of the world.

One day a spotted leopard named Lester happened to witness an albino leopard overtake and neatly fell a swift young gazelle. "My, my," Lester said admiringly, "that was done with extraordinary speed and skill. I wonder what kind of animal that is. It looks like a leopard, but it couldn't be a true leopard without any spots."

CHARLES MERRILL SMITH

104

It so happened that Lester was a big land owner and an astute businessman. It occurred to him that if he could persuade some of these albinos to come and work for him he wouldn't have to chase gazelles himself, and maybe the albinos could catch enough gazelles that Lester could turn a nice profit selling gazelle meat to other leopards. So he sweet-talked the albinos into working for him, which wasn't hard, as the albinos, remember, were naive and tended to believe anything a prosperous business leopard told them.

Pretty soon the other spotted leopards saw that Lester was on to a good thing, so they went out and got themselves some albinos to do their work, and before long the spotted leopard colony had almost as many albinos residing in it as spotted leopards. Some of the albinos went into business for themselves, and others decided to run for political office, and then the trouble began.

"We all gotta do somethin' about these here white leopards," George Spotted Leopard, who was governor of the colony, said one day, "or they all gonna claim e-quality with spotted leopards." So Lester and George and some of the leading business and professional spotted leopards got together and drew up some instant traditions governing white-spotted relationships. These traditions were about what you would imagine—white leopards could live only in certain areas, could hold only a limited list of jobs (mostly menial), had to get off the jungle trails in deference to spotted leopards, things like that.

Some spotted leopards who prided themselves on being liberals protested. "After all, even though they are white they are indubitably leopards," they said.

"They all may be leopards," George Spotted Leopard said,

"but would you want your daughter to mate with one of them?"

Even the liberal leopards found this idea repugnant and helped pass laws forbidding miscegenation. (However, since female albino leopards were reputed to be very amorous, it was accepted that male spotted leopards could sneak into albino town for an evening of recreation so long as they were decently surreptitious about it.)

The albino leopards didn't take this lying down. Dr. Tom White Leopard, who had the largest medical practice among his own leopards, said, "We've got it pretty good, we'd better be content with gradual progress." But Bobby White Leopard, who was a radical, organized a group of militants, named them the White Panthers, and proclaimed that white is beautiful, white is superior, and bombed spotted leopard institutions and shot it out with spotted leopard police and generally disrupted the peace.

"We oughta ship all them albinos back to where they come from," Governor George Spotted Leopard would proclaim, and then the spotted leopards would elect him for another term of office. White leopards had to go to inferior schools and couldn't compete with spotted leopards for good jobs, and many of them had to go on welfare, so they didn't make much social progress. Spotted leopards pointed to the poor educational and economic levels achieved by white leopards and said, "See, they are inferior or they would work hard and be successful just like us." This was considered impeccable logic in spotted leopard society.

But Bobby White Leopard and his militant pals would answer this argument with White Panther logic. "We gonna take over, and then there will be justice for all the leopards,

CHARLES MERRILL SMITH

106

even if we have to shoot a lot of spotted leopards to attain it," they would say.

So things are a mess in the leopard colony, although the spotted leopards still have the upper hand, and the albino leopards still have to take the worst jobs and live in albino ghettos, and it will be a long time before albinos will be accepted as the equal of spotteds.

MORAL: *In this world it is usually an advantage to be white, but not always.*

Submit this, if You will, Sir, to Your Heavenly Council for its consideration. If these saints and angels can figure out a solution to the color problem, please let us hear about it, because, as of right now, no one down here seems to have a clue as to how we can solve it.

23

• How Much Should I Depend on You?

Everlasting Arms, Sir . . . From my earliest Sunday school memories on I have been taught that the main thing about You is that when life gets to be too much for me You will be quick to help me handle it. Nothing is too much for You. You are the Everlasting Arms on which I can always lean for support. All I have to do to qualify for this cosmic aid program is to love You, praise You, and give You the credit.

I must say that the concept of Everlasting Arms, ever ready to catch me when I stumble, a divine manager who will rectify my human errors, is one of the most appealing pictures of Your nature extant.

As I have mentioned previously, I believe Your world is a good world. However, living in it does entail some fierce problems.

So often, for example, even though I think I am pretty smart, my wisdom is inadequate for the decisions I have to make. It is nice to know, in such exigencies, that You will guide me.

Or take the matter of the messes I get myself into—sometimes inadvertently, sometimes through stupidity, sometimes through greed or selfishness or pride. Usually, when I can't unravel the situation by myself I resort, as You know, to calling on You to rescue me.

Some theologians, in fact, say that this sense of dependence on You is the very heart and essence of religion. Many of our best-loved Christian hymns express the sentiment that though we are frail and inadequate to cope with the stiff demands life makes of us, with Your help we can overcome. Most of us, me included, like it this way.

But awhile back I read something that the late Dietrich Bonhoeffer said. Bonhoeffer, who must have been one of Your favorites, being a modern martyr who died for having the courage of his convictions, and was a serious Christian if there ever was one, said something to the effect that, "Perhaps it is God's will for us to live in the world as men without God."

Well, Sir, when I first read this it appalled me. I thought it was downright blasphemous. But I couldn't get it out of my mind. Could You possibly want me to do battle with the world, the flesh, and the devil as if You didn't exist? Would You leave me all alone to face the frightening possibilities of life?

Then I got to thinking—Jesus told us to understand You as the perfect father. Now I am a father too, although by no means a perfect one. How is a good father supposed to treat his children?

Does he encourage them to depend on him to solve every problem, heal every wound, extricate them from all difficulties? It would be a very bad father who treated his children after this fashion. He would keep them juveniles forever. They would never mature and become persons in their own right. There would be no moral or spiritual fiber in them.

As a matter of fact, I know parents who approach parenthood this way. I know middle-aged men who are dominated by strong-willed fathers. Though they are gray and paunchy they are children still. They are pathetic, objects of the world's sniggering laughter.

Is this what Bonhoeffer had in mind when he made that rather outrageous remark? Is my analogy of a good earthly father appropriate to understanding Your ways? When I face a personal crisis or am flattened by despair, I instinctively turn to You and plead for help. I probably always will do this. But should I catch myself and say to myself, "Look here, your Heavenly Father wants you to act like a grown-up man, expects you to show your love for Him by depending on yourself"?

I would prefer to believe that You want to rush to my aid whenever I get in over my depth. It is a disturbing thought that those Everlasting Arms in which I have so long trusted might not be there to catch me.

But maybe I'll be a spiritually healthier, more mature person if I learn to live in the world as a man without God.

Sir, which way is it? I need the answer, but I hear none. But, as someone has observed, sometimes God speaks in silences.

Maybe that is your answer.

CHARLES MERRILL SMITH

24

Is "Loss of Faith" Always a Loss?

Source of Our Faith, Sir . . . I don't know if You do much television watching in heaven, although considering the dopey stuff it presents as entertainment I would guess that You don't. However, occasionally one sees something on the tube which provokes interest and reflection.

For example, I saw this interview with Patricia Neal, the Oscar-winning movie star. You may recall that a few years ago she was felled by three massive strokes. Even the most optimistic prognosis consigned her to a state of a semivegetable for life. But, amazingly, she has fought her way back to health and has resumed her acting career.

What I want to take up with You is a statement she made. She said that before her stroke she was "very religious," but afterwards, when she regained consciousness, she discovered that she wasn't religious anymore. This sudden absence of faith could be ascribed to bitterness over her misfortune. You have witnessed many people, I'm sure, reject You after some personal misfortune because "I don't want anything to do with a God who would do this to me."

That isn't the case with Miss Neal. She said she regretted her sudden loss of faith and hoped she would be religious again.

This interview generated a number of thoughts on the subject of religious faith. Let me share some of them with You.

For one thing, Miss Neal reversed the almost standard sequence of emotions reported by people who suffer a severe clout from life and then recover. Such people usually report that their traumatic experience intensifies their faith. Since God has brought them through the storm to a safe harbor they have seen the light.

What happened, then, in Miss Neal's case? It's not that she is bitter or sorry for herself. She exhibits a glowing gratitude that she has come through a bout with the grim reaper when he almost had her down for the count. She is glad to be alive as, I suppose, only a person who thought she wouldn't be can be glad.

Furthermore, she overflows with praise for her husband, friends, neighbors who gave themselves without reservation to help her struggle back to life. There is no indication that she is mad at You for permitting all this agony to be her portion. This kind of glowing, thankful joy that she has made it through the valley of the shadow, coupled with a loss of religious faith, is something new in my fairly lengthy acquaintance with the varieties and subspecies of religious experience.

CHARLES MERRILL SMITH

Is there a hint of an answer in the fact that Miss Neal also lost her ability to speak, and had to be reeducated to associate people and objects with their correct names? Is this an indication to us that there is a portion of the brain which controls the thoughts, feelings, emotions, convictions, etc. which come under the label "religious" just as there are brain centers which govern speech?

If such is the case, then Christian evangelism is going about its business the hard way. We could make people religious by learning how to develop the proper neurons or synapses or whatever it is that connects us with our religious motor. (I am, I confess, a little weak in clinical psychology, but You will understand what I am getting at.)

If this is how it really is, then our Christian seminaries should jettison their departments of preaching, teaching, and counseling. They are outdated. What they need is one big department of clinical pastoral psychology which would turn out pastors equipped to develop the correct neural connections to give people a powerful faith. It is a revolting thought, I admit, but logical if given the premise.

I am certain that thousands, maybe millions, of people who heard Miss Neal confess that she isn't religious anymore will think this a tragedy. For a few weeks after her TV confession the postman no doubt staggered up to her mail box each morning with a kind of mail with which I have become well acquainted since I have, from time to time, appeared on TV interviews and talk shows discussing religion.

There will be some kindly letters from well-meaning people who will give her guaranteed formulas for recovering her religion. Mostly, these will be from the gentler type of Christian fundamentalist and will inform her that by giving her heart to Jesus, adopting an uncomplicated belief in the absolute accuracy of the Holy Scriptures (King James Version), and a structuring of her life with the values of rural American Protestantism she can recapture her departed religiousness.

Some mail will tell her, at length and plentifully embroidered with quotations, encyclicals, and dubious theological arguments that the path to salvation is the road to Rome.

Other letters will be hostile, nasty, abusive. There is a type of religious personality which gets its kicks out of a violent denunciation of those who do not think as they think. I am sure You deplore this kind of twisted and truculent faith, Sir, but Miss Neal is bound to hear from these people.

One of the reasons I am certain she will hear from them is that she smoked a cigarette during the interview, and also mentioned that she favors martini cocktails. So she can expect to receive no small number of epistles telling her that no wonder she has lost her religion, tobacco-puffing and cocktail-swilling hussy that she is. If she wants to get right with You, these letters will say, she had better cut out these sinful self-indulgences.

Many of these vituperative letters will come in envelopes bulging with tracts. These tracts, crudely written, full of misspellings, will be on subjects such as why You want us to wipe every Communist off the face of the earth in the name of Christ, or seventeen proofs from the Bible that white Protestants are Your chosen people, or how every Jew is plotting to destroy Christian America. I have enough of these things to start a tract store, and so will she before long.

None of this, though, is the point of my communication.

CHARLES MERRILL SMITH

What I am wondering is whether You consider Miss Neal's loss of faith really a loss.

You would know, of course, what kind of religion she once had but has no more. She didn't enlighten the viewing audience as to its nature. Was it a "faith in faith"? Was it a shallow mysticism masquerading as Christianity? Was it a conformity to the cultus of some sect or other? Was it a sweet Jesusology? These are what people frequently mean when they say they are "very religious."

Would You agree with me, Sir, that if any one or a combination of these is what she lost, then her loss is really a gain? I look on it as a gain if she is rid of a cheap, junky, unreal faith which could only have been a burden and not a blessing, whether she knew it or not. Phony faith, however comforting for the moment, is a barrier to authentic relations with the Ultimate. Or so it seems to me.

She is the gainer by her loss of faith (assuming it was a junky faith that she lost) because there was no possibility that she would have moved on to a genuine, life-giving faith until she cleared out the clutter of ersatz religion. There is no assurance that she will move on to the real thing, of course. But that is at least now an option for her which did not exist before.

The point of Miss Neal's story, as I read it, is that the abandonment of a state of being "very religious" is not necessarily a spiritual tragedy, that loss of one's faith is not always a loss but sometimes a gain.

Personally, I have never experienced a precipitant, dramatic departure of a once-cherished belief such as was visited on Miss Neal. But I know what it is like to lose one's faith by a

HOW TO TALK TO GOD . . .

gradual but radical shift in religious perspective, if by loss of faith one means discarding what he formerly clung to in favor of a clearer spiritual insight. I'd like to tell Miss Neal that the loss can be uncomfortable because no one abandons what he once viewed as certainties without pain. But she knows that already. What I would also tell her is that the gain far outweighs the loss.

People who say, "I have the same unshakeable, unchanging faith today that I had as a child," usually act as if someone ought to step forward and present them with a morocco-bound, gold-stamped Bible for a prize. How anyone can live in the real world, be involved at all with life, and not make constant adjustments to his faith in the light of experience—which is a form of the loss of faith—is beyond me. Didn't St. Paul recommend somewhere that adults can profitably dispense with childish things?

Anyway, Miss Neal's experience of the loss of faith sounds to me like an unfinished parable with the flavor of the kind of story Jesus told.

Is that how You read it?

CHARLES MERRILL SMITH

25

The Dull Gray Prison of the Literal Mind

Creator of Joy, Sir . . . Once when I was teaching a class of adult laymen, one of the students asked the question, "How can I find joy in my religion?"

Well, Sir, I thought this was a terribly sad question, not to mention an unintentional criticism of You. I mean, if You are the source of our faith, as we claim, and as the Bible says You are, then what kind of a God are You whose followers look on their religion as a lugubrious business? This question is only another way of saying, "I find Christianity a boring religion, and I don't think it ought to be, and I'd like to get some fun out of it."

I have read my Harnack on the history of Christianity, and I recall his observation that the early Christians, despite dungeon, fire, and sword, being fed to the lions, and a host of

117

other unpleasant experiences, were—as Harnack put it—"absurdly happy." No one, so far as I know, is saying this about modern Christians.

Now I'm not blaming You. I don't think of You as a celestial ogre or I wouldn't be talking to You as I am. But don't You think You ought to do something about it? Or, rather, we Christians ought to do something about it.

But what?

I don't pretend to understand all the reasons for the joyless quality of contemporary Christianity. One reason, I suspect, is the literal mindedness which, as I see it, is the special curse of the standard brand Protestant Christian.

In fact, I sometimes wish the Bible had never been written, although I know this is heresy indeed. I don't really wish it because then there wouldn't be any Christianity. But You have to admit that this fundamentally beautiful, imaginative book (or, more accurately, portable library), rich in poetry and vivid narrative, has been much abused in Your name.

Are You aware, Sir, that the average, man-in-the-pew type of Christians today believe the Bible to be the ultimate authority in matters of faith and life, but they hardly ever read it? Most of us, I'm afraid, have only a vague acquaintance with the Bible. What we do have is a semisuperstitious, sentimental attitude toward it. We think of it as a sacred book in some sense which we don't understand, written by You, word-for-word. We are convinced that every part of the Bible down to the last "thee," "thou," and "begat" must be viewed as the inerrant and literal word from Your office.

I can't prove that You didn't do it this way, of course, but if You did I would feel justified in entering a demurrer. There must be a better way. Any concept of the Scriptures which reduces Isaiah, Jeremiah, St. Paul, or the author of the Johannine literature to the status of male secretary jotting down what You dictate leaves me pretty cold.

But I'm off my subject. This view of the Bible produces in people who don't really know what it says and have no intention of finding out a feeling that it is full of grim and restrictive admonitions from You as to how they must behave which, if faithfully adhered to, would turn them into a person somewhat like their pious, juiceless, maiden aunt. Since very few people want to be like their pious, juiceless, maiden aunt, they never connect Christianity with the idea of joy.

This biblical literal-mindedness insists that the creation stories in Genesis (Why did You think it necessary to include two creation stories? Wouldn't one have been enough?) must be accepted as scientifically accurate and historically exact accounts of Your creative activity.

I have heard biblical literalists defend the Book of Jonah as history, although anyone not infected with literalism can't help but perceive that it is an inspired, witty, short story, a satire on the narrow-mindedness and racial prejudice of the Jews at that particular point in time.

Literalists look on the pictorial details of paradise described in Revelation as a photograph of the hereafter. They even try to contort the Sermon on the Mount into a set of specific, organized rules, an ethical prescription. We could multiply the illustrations.

It seems to me, Sir, that this kind of literalistic approach to the source book of our faith creates a dull gray prison of the mind, locking out the exciting possibilities, the stimulating insights, the genuine revelations about You and about the potentials for man's life—all of which are necessary prerequisites to a joyous faith.

What we have ended up with, I fear, is a faith which shackles the spirit. Who can enjoy a faith like that? It is a burden to carry a penal code imposed by a grim deity who occupies himself devising ways to make us pay for any fun we might have.

Theoretically I'm certain You never intended for us to envisage You as a spiritual policeman. On the other hand, a lot of us who have shed our traditional literalistic views haven't entirely escaped a sneaking fear that You are watching us with a beady eye. We have difficulty shaking off a suspicion that You don't really want us to be joyous, and that You will exact a penalty if we are.

For example, I have a wide acquaintance among the clergy, most of whom abandoned literalism a long time ago. But not a few of these guys, though they want to be normal, joyful people, just can't make it. They are haunted and hedged in by their early training that a Christian must be solemn, somber, and pious or You will fix him good—if not here, then in the life hereafter. They know better intellectually, but they can't break the bonds of their emotional conditioning.

Such people often have a quality of antiseptic goodness about them, which passes quite adequately in Christian culture for Christian virtue. But they are really miserable. They have internal conflicts You wouldn't believe. They plod through life as Christian automatons, but they get ulcers and other uncomfortable diseases stemming from a troubled spirit. This just can't be what You want of us.

I might as well confess that if I were convinced that the Christian faith demanded that I live in the dull gray prison of the literal mind, that in order to please You I had to conform to the joyless, narrow, life-denying, pious Protestant image of the Christian man, I would junk the whole effort and be a happy pagan.

Are You familiar, Sir, with Wordsworth's lines which he wrote in reaction to the grubby Christianity he saw all about him?

> Great God! I'd rather be a pagan
> Suckled in a creed outworn,
> That might I, standing on this pleasant lea
> Have glimpses that would make me less forlorn,
> Have sight of Proteus, rising from the sea,
> Or hear old Triton blow his wreathèd horn.

Well, that's how I feel, Sir, about the dull gray Christian (I use the term loosely) prison of the literal mind. We keep talking about how the gospel is good news. But what's good news about a religion which wants me to live in a spiritual jail with You as warden? That's bad news to me. Good news is news of liberty and joy, news that I should expand my humanness instead of contract it.

If the literalists are right, then I expect I'm in trouble with You for talking this way, and that You won't let me off easy for harboring such blasphemous thoughts.

But I'm betting they are wrong. Anyway, I'm willing to take my chances.

HOW TO TALK TO GOD . . .

26

You Won't Believe This One

Genial Spirit, Sir . . . Does the population of heaven need a good laugh, or at least a hearty chuckle, now and then? If so, You could call this little story to their attention.

A news item from somewhere in England relates that the winner of the Sunday school Scripture-reading contest in a certain village is a lad by the name of Nigel Perfect. Can You believe that? If his name had been Percival Perfect I would have said it was a put-on, that no one could be named Percival Perfect and win a Scripture-reading contest. But Nigel Perfect is credible, although just barely.

Nigel Perfect sounds like a character in an old-fashioned melodrama. The poor kid will have to go through life dragging the dead weight of this execrable name with him.

But to win a Scripture-reading contest is really too much for a lad named Nigel Perfect. It makes one wonder if there is a self-fulfilling power in names (Dr. Goodspeed, the great Bible translator and scholar, and William Temple, distinguished churchman and theologian, come to mind). Did young Nigel, bright-eyed and downy-cheeked, say to himself in the depths of his id, "Perfect I am, perfect I will be," and then structure his ego so that his satisfactions are produced by living up to his name?

If a kindly but whimsical providence spares me for another thirty years, I confidently expect to read that the Very Reverend Dr. Nigel Perfect has become the youngest Archbishop of Canterbury in the history of the Church of England. Without doubt, Nigel Perfect will launch a career in the church, this being the only profession suitable for a chap with a name like that.

And he will go far in the church. In fact, he can't miss. What congregation in its right mind would pass up the chance to say "our pastor is Perfect"?

I do feel sorry for his wife, though, don't You?

27

Should I Sell My Stock in First National City Bank?

Prudent and Tolerant Spirit, Sir . . . I find myself faced with one of those little ethical dilemmas which nag at me like a lone and unlocatable mosquito in a dark room. Let me lay it before You.

Without doubt You are as upset as I am with the government of South Africa. One doesn't have to be very sensitive morally to be revolted by the cruel and inhuman racial policies of this government. What makes it all the worse is that these guys are all upright Dutch Reformed Protestant Christians and they claim their cruelty to the colored people whose land they stole is Your design and Your will.

Well, anyway, South Africa has many promising investment opportunities, and many American banks have money on loan to the government at most profitable terms. One of them

124

is the First National City Bank of New York, and I hold stock in that bank.

Actually, I have four shares of the bank stock. It started out as one share, but stocks have a way of growing, like an amoeba, by splitting and then splitting again, so now I have four shares. A dividend check for ninety cents or so comes in annually or semiannually, I forget which, a portion of which presumably is attributable to interest on the bank's loan to the government of South Africa.

A part of my income, therefore, is derived from the misery of the natives of South Africa. This would be the moral equivalent, I suppose, of owning an interest in a plantation which profited by slave labor.

What would You suggest I do about it, Sir?

Would it be better for me to hang on to the stock and write letters of protest to the bank's officers? How much attention is the board of directors going to pay to a four-share stockholder? Would selling the stock and washing my hands of the bank's ethically dubious enterprise in South Africa satisfy the demands of Christian behavior?

The trouble is, life is full of these pestiferous little ethical problems.

I buy products whose advertising I abhor as tasteless, offensive, misleading, or downright dishonest because I like the product itself. I trade at a chain grocery market which practices medieval employment policies rather than inconvenience myself to seek out a less offensive establishment. I drive an automobile whose maker profits by polluting the environment. I purchase books from a denominational pub-

HOW TO TALK TO GOD . . .

CENTRAL CHRISTIAN CHURCH
ELKHART, INDIANA

lisher which has a shabby record as to its labor policies, and whose business methods I know for a fact come pretty close to being crooked. The fresh fruits and vegetables I enjoy so much come to me courtesy of the degredation and hopelessness of the people who pick them. Almost everything I do, so far as the daily trivia of living is concerned, is splashed with sin.

So what is a man of Christian conscience to do?

Perhaps one could fashion a life-style which is consistently Christian and uninvolved with the sins of others, but it wouldn't be easy.

Can I be free of culpability by saying, "I don't cheat, misrepresent, or oppress people, and therefore I share no guilt of those who do, even though I do business with them"?

I once knew a church in a town whose only industry was making whiskey bottles. The church had a law which prevented any member from "either using or profiting from the sale of alcoholic beverages." Most of the church's members drew their paychecks from the bottle plant, and even the preacher's salary derived in large part from the same source. But no one was troubled by this. Even though everyone knew what went into the bottles, they said they were selling glass, not booze.

Technically they were correct, of course. But doesn't the argument smack of sophistry to You? Such splitting of ethical hairs, however, is one common Christian way out of these plaguing moral dilemmas. To me, though, it sounds very much like Pilate refusing to rule on the case of Jesus because it wasn't his problem.

CHARLES MERRILL SMITH

Back to my First National City Bank stocks. I should make it clear that they aren't actually mine; they belong to my wife. She inherited the one share, and her name alone is on the four fancy certificates to which the one has grown. I couldn't sell them if I wanted to. She's the one who'll have to make the decision. It is no concern of mine.

28

Where Are the New Myths?

Omniscient Sir . . . Are the works of Dr. Harvey Cox popular in heaven?

My slight personal contact with Dr. Cox almost wrecked my image of the Baptist clergy. He is a card-carrying Baptist clergyman, all right, so according to my image of this ecclesiastical breed he should be a black-suited, white-shirted man with the middle-aged manners and impeccable piety of a small-town undertaker. All my training and experience (until recently) has led me to believe that this is what Baptists insist on in their clergy, which is a compliment to the Baptists, or an insult, depending on your point of view.

Well, I couldn't have been more wrong. Dr. Cox is a young-ish man with a beard and a casual intellectual insouciance which is quite charming. He is attached to the Harvard Divinity School, carrying the impressive title of "professor of theology and culture," but unlike most high-level scholars he doesn't appear terribly impressed with himself. For all I know he is terribly impressed with himself, but I give him points for concealing it.

Dr. Cox writes articles for learned theological journals. He frequently writes articles for *Playboy* magazine, which isn't exactly a theological journal but sometimes seems to mistake itself for one. And he writes books which sell in the hundreds of thousands, and not very many theologians can do that.

Anyway, at the moment I am intrigued by one of Dr. Cox's theories about the church. He thinks that organized religion will continue its present decline because there isn't any steam left in the old myths by which the church lived so vigorously in the past. These old Hebrew-Christian myths from which, up until recently, we derived our understanding of the world and the values by which we fashioned our lives, no longer have much power over the imagination of modern man—or so Dr. Cox claims.

Unfortunately, he says, the church goes on telling the old story (myths) in the traditional and accepted manner which accomplishes nothing except stirring a few beloved memories and convincing the already convinced. This leaves the church playing the role of a quaint historical society made up mostly of people who like that sort of thing. But quaint historical societies do not command the allegiance of busy, troubled, questioning, puzzled people looking for the words of life. Quaint historical societies do not save the world.

Dr. Cox could be wrong, of course. After all, he isn't You, so he isn't omniscient. But I have this hunch that he has put his finger on something pretty important. If I understand what he is saying, it is that the essential proclamation of, say, the Adam and Eve story (which is the proclamation that You created the universe) is still as valid as it was when those unknown authors of Genesis put it together in the Eden myth, but that we can't tell it that way any more and expect anyone to pay much attention.

When this idea becomes common knowledge among Christians, if it ever does, a lot of people are going to be pretty upset. I'm not sure but that it makes me, who fancies himself an open-minded man, a little uneasy.

What would You advise us to do about it, Sir?

One thing we could do is to defend the old myths. We could play Horatius at the bridge and stoutly defend the old battle line. Not a few people would rally to such a campaign. In fact, much of what we call mass evangelism and a great deal of self-designated "conservative Christianity" uses its ammunition defending old myths, and not without some measure of popular success. But it seems to me, Sir, that the world treats this sort of thing pretty much as Hitler's panzer divisions treated the Maginot Line—it ignores it.

Another way to handle the problem posed by the passing of the old myths is to pretend that the church is essentially a spiritual self-help society. If it is that, if the Christian church has nothing to do with man's relation to the contemporary world, no concern for the values by which he relates to the world, then it doesn't need any myths at all.

Many people already believe this is how the church should view itself. They are convinced that the church should be a spiritual refuge from the world of war and crime and drugs and racial strife and all the troubles of daily existence. This is the way our most prosperous and successful suburban churches operate. It strikes me, though, that this is a strategy comparable to hearing that your house is on fire and coping with the unpleasant reality by quietly getting drunk.

Would You agree with me, Sir, that the proper mission of the church is to proclaim the eternal truth rather than defend the old myths?

This, though, is the source of my unease over the passing of the old myths. The good word that You love me and forgive me is as relevant today as it was to the citizens of first-century Palestine. But we don't live in first-century Palestine, so the myths which moved it don't grab us. Or more to the point, we don't even live in rural nineteenth-century America, and the myths which generated so much heat in the camp meeting or little brown church in the vale leave us cold.

So if the eternal truths must be reclothed in new myths, who is going to do it, Sir? If I knew how to remythologize the Christian faith so as to get the Christian message across to an age which is indifferent to the old myths, I would be the hottest thing in prophets there is.

But I don't know how. Where are the new Christian myths we apparently need so desperately? You might give the problem some thought.

29

Stop the World! I Want to Stay On

Perpetually Creative Spirit, Sir . . . I consider myself a very worldly guy, and I'm sure You approve because in the New Testament You told us that You love the world, so I'm just being godly when I love it too.

But lately I'm constantly assailed by a conviction that in the race to keep up with the world I'm going to lose. So if You could manage to slow it down a little, just enough that I can continue to hang on, I'd be most grateful. Sometimes I think the world asks an awful lot of me, devoted as I am to it.

What I'm really asking is that the world will hold still long enough for me to assimilate everything it throws at me.

Take an example, Sir. You've probably noticed that I'm a sports fan. Things were just fine when I could follow baseball in the spring and summer, football in the fall, and basketball during the winter, with very little overlapping, a rememberable number of teams, and only an infrequent golf match or hockey game to divert my interest from the mainline spectator sports.

Now the seasons stretch well-nigh the year around, teams proliferate like rabbits, new leagues pop up all over the place, and there are so many players I can't possibly keep track of them. Things are so bad that, what with the pro basketball playoffs, the Stanley Cup series, and the opening of baseball season all more or less coinciding, I haven't seen Henry Aaron hit a homer yet this year, which is comparable to visiting the Vatican without looking in on the Sistine Chapel. I'm feeling pretty depressed about it.

I suppose one can live the rich, full life even if he has to miss some of the sports action. Books, though, are another thing entirely.

I've known for years that I was getting behind in my reading. I comforted myself for awhile by telling myself that when we got the children raised and launched into the world there would be plenty of time to catch up. But it hasn't worked out that way. Oh, I keep at it, Sir, but I feel like a man bailing a leaky boat in a heavy storm. No matter how hard I try I can't keep ahead of the rising waters.

The trouble is, Sir—in case You hadn't noticed—that along with the torrent of trash, the cascade of significant, worthwhile, important books gets larger all the time.

For example, my knowledge of the existentialists is full of holes, not because the information isn't readily available but because I haven't gotten around to patching them up.

HOW TO TALK TO GOD . . .

I've hardly dipped my beak into the works of Pierre Teilhard de Chardin. What I don't know about the modern poets is a lot. I have shamelessly neglected the field of the mystery novel, a minor but intellectually respectable and most rewarding branch of literature in which I was once quite knowledgeable.

I feel a need to know more about international affairs. Loving something also means knowing it, and if I am to love the world as You have indicated I should, I ought to know it better than I do. Most of us know and love our own little corner of the world, which isn't at all what You had in mind, I suspect, when You told us to love it.

I want to travel, but even if I had the money and with the jet age and all, it still takes a lot of time to see Afghanistan, Outer Mongolia, the Australian Outback, and—now that the Ping-Pong team has been there—mainland China.

Also, I yearn to master the piano, learn French, see the paintings in the Hermitage, write a book on Jonathan Swift, take a trip on a tramp steamer, become a skilled chess player, and brush up my New Testament Greek. If I could find the time, I would relish teaching myself French cooking and trying my hand at painting. In addition, I have long believed I have the makings of a first-rate poet, but I haven't gotten around to working at it. This is only a partial list.

What I'm saying is that I'm greedy for life, hungry for new experiences, a glutton for tasting what the world has to offer. But the world keeps offering me more and more and more. I would gorge myself on it if I could, but it goes so fast I can't keep up.

Should I scale down my expectations? Would I be happier

CHARLES MERRILL SMITH

134

and better adjusted if I let my dreams and fantasies recede until they are congruent with my capacities? Or should my reach for life exceed my grasp?

These are questions they don't deal with in Sunday school, but they ought to. Meanwhile, I have this feeling that if You could just bring the world to a halt or at least a slow walk for a while I could get abreast of it.

Do You get a lot of complaints along this line?

30

Should I Accept a Blended Religion?

Tolerant Spirit, Sir . . . When I was a teenager I attended the Epworth League. Now anyone who even remembers the Epworth League has seen better days. The Epworth League is what the Methodist church called its youth organization many years ago.

The league was organized and designed to educate postadolescents about You, curb our more effervescent instincts by teaching us that to let them bubble and fizz was sinful, and to hammer us into reasonable replicas of the ideal Methodist Christian personality—not necessarily in that order of importance.

Its main attraction for me, I'm afraid, wasn't spiritual. The Epworth League in our town, for reasons I cannot recall at this late date, attracted the best-looking girls. We had lots of Presbyterian and Baptist boys in our Epworth League, not to mention a few Roman Catholics and Seventh-Day Adventists.

Well, anyway, we had to have a lesson before we could make our connection for the evening. The one topic I remember from Epworth League, probably because it came up with frequency, was the question, "Will the heathens who never heard of Christ be saved?" I can't for the life of me tell You why we debated it because it couldn't have been a burning issue to us, but we did.

Odd, isn't it, Sir, that in a slightly different form it is a burning, or at least a smoldering issue for Christians today?

It looks to me as if we are moving toward a religion which is a blend of many religions. We are adulterating our Christianity with teachings and insights from Buddhism, Islam, and any other source which appeals to us. Kids today really go for mystical Eastern religions, and like to mix it up with whatever parts of the Christian faith they particularly like. The word for this religious stew, I know, is "eclectic," but I hesitate to use it lest You suspect me of intellectual pride, which I know You don't like.

My questions, Sir: Should I accept as valid these blends of Christianity and other religions? Is a blended religion a good thing or a bad thing?

You may wish to point out to me that we have already adulterated the Christian faith without any help from other religions. I guess I couldn't argue that. Quite a number of theologians have told us how we mix nationalism, middle-class cultural ideals, American economic beliefs, and who knows what else with Christianity and have come up with an agglomeration which would cause St. Paul to wince.

But that is another problem. In spite of these non-Christian accretions, we have continued to believe that the Christian faith is in some way unique.

Sir, is it unique, or isn't it? That's what I need to know.

On the one hand, to insist that it is doesn't make much sense. Did Jesus actually say that no one could come to You except through him? Or was this something that some unknown editor wrote in that he said because the editor thought Jesus would have said it if he had thought about it? This wouldn't be a problem for a biblical literalist, of course, because the literalist can't question the authenticity of anything in the Scriptures, even the parts where little children's brains are beaten out against stones for Your greater glory. But I am not a biblical literalist, and I know someone had to edit the Gospels, and being a writer I know what editors can and usually do to original manuscripts. My guess is that Jesus never said such a thing, and I hope You won't consider my opinion heretical.

The conviction that our religion is unique also breeds some rather unpleasant attitudes. For example, we find it almost impossible to think of our religion as unique without at the same time thinking of it as superior to all other religions.

Sir, if You will pull my dossier from the heavenly files or computer memory bank, or from whatever You keep it in, You will discover that I have a rather commendable record in the support of foreign missions. I have given liberally to the missions enterprise of the church, pushed it hard in sermons, and devised clever ways of raising money for it. You can't fault me on this one.

I was raised to believe that a church which didn't major in

missions support wasn't much of a church. I always set as a goal for the churches I served a fifty-fifty division of the budget—as much for missions as for our local expenses. We never made it. You surely know, Sir, how difficult church finances can be. You have to pay the janitor and the light bill to stay in business. You don't have to pay the missions apportionment. So if the budget falls short it is easiest to skimp a little on missions. But I tried.

Anyway, in spite of my enthusiasm for foreign missions and stalwart support of it, I always was troubled a little by the philosophy behind it. We Christians believe that "we've a story to tell to the nations," but we never entertained the thought that the nations had anything important to say to us. There is a spiritual arrogance in this attitude which I find distasteful. Yet if Christianity is unique, if it can do something for a person which no other religion can do, the attitude is sound. It poses, for me, a distressing spiritual dilemma.

On the other hand, if Christianity is just another of the great world religions, good, helpful, worthwhile, but not unique, why should I go to the trouble of exporting it? Why not be happy with my Christ and leave the Arab undisturbed with his Prophet Mohammed? Why say to the Hindu, "Look, you ought to accept Christ"?

Now, Sir, You have probably noticed that the missions emphasis is shifting from persuasion to dialogue. Except for the fundamentalists (who still do it the old way) the modern missionary is unlikely to say to the heathen, the Hindu, or even the native in the African bush, "You must accept Christ to be saved." What he says is, "Let's sit down and talk—you tell me what you think about God and I'll tell you how I see it."

I have this odd feeling, though, that while the modern approach is more Christian in spirit than the old-fashioned save-their-souls method, it isn't going to be easy to keep a missionary program going in order to carry on group discussions about the relative merits of Christianity and other religions.

Sometimes, Sir, I wish I didn't have to make sense out of everything. I wish I could just accept great chunks of faith on faith or authority and be quit of pondering whether there is any logic to it or not. But my mind doesn't work that way. I have to see that things hang together before I can believe. Since You are the creator of my mind I don't see how You can hold this against me.

However, whether it is a holdover from my lifelong training or not I don't know, but I can't quite give up the idea that Jesus is unique.

I'm not yet ready to accept a blended religion. I'm ready to listen, I hope, without arrogant impatience, to what the proponents of other religions have to tell me. Actually, I'm rather eager to hear what they have to say. But, at this point anyway, I'm going to talk back on the assumption that no matter how many good, helpful, inspiring insights the other guy has to offer through his religion, Christianity still has something to offer him that he can't get anywhere else.

Now, Sir, I think I should lay off talking to him about the incarnation. I hope You won't mind. After all, the other guy isn't going to buy that unless he is a simple, credulous type who has no trouble believing anything anybody tells him.

The incarnation, as explicated by Christian theologians, may

CHARLES MERRILL SMITH

140

well be the way You did it. But it rests on the authority of the Scriptures, and non-Christians don't accept the authority of the Christian Scriptures. I, for one, am not prepared to tell them that they have to accept them or go to hell, and I doubt if You would sanction such an approach either.

What I am prepared to do is to claim that Jesus shows us in a way no one else ever has what it means to be truly human. I can, in good conscience, say to him, "Here is the only man who ever got his values straight, who ordered life's priorities as God intended them to be ordered."

I know, of course, that my approach dispenses with the Christ-as-mystical-savior idea which we find in St. Paul's writings and which is so dear to the hearts of evangelists. My method throws out the sawdust-trail, make-a-decision-for Christ, sign-a-card-that-you-are-saved paraphernalia which is so much a part of our American Protestant Christian culture. The intelligent Buddhist wouldn't care. What does he know about traditional American Christian evangelistic methods anyway?

But he will be interested in something which, simply, shows him how to live more truly as a human being at his best. This, I believe, has a universal appeal.

I don't even say my intelligent Hindu has to become a Baptist or a Presbyterian or some other brand of Christian, although all too often that was the unadmitted motive behind much Christian missionary activity. And there is no denying that the denominational statistical game we American Christians play brought out the dollars for mission programs.

All I want to do is to show him the uniqueness of Christ as I conceive that uniqueness.

Is that enough? Will my way put ample emphasis on Christianity's uniqueness and at the same time promote a Christian openness to what the other fellow has to say to me? Can I hold this position without spiritual arrogance?

In short, Sir, do You buy my thinking on this subject?

P.S. I still haven't quite figured out how the heathen who has never heard of Christ is to be saved, but I'll keep working on it.

CHARLES MERRILL SMITH

31

Will I Meet Hitler in Heaven?

Benevolent and Forgiving Spirit, Sir . . . I doubt if You subscribe to *Playboy* magazine, and I don't either. But occasionally I buy a copy, not to look at the pictures I hasten to assure You, but because of some article in it I want to read (I admit it isn't easy to skip all the pictures when you turn to where the article is continued, and some of those pictures are lulus, but I don't want to get into that.).

The article I wanted to read in a current issue was a *Playboy* interview with Albert Speer, Hitler's number one man in the Third Reich.

Speer, who has had twenty years in prison to think over his role as Hitler's best buddy, has now repented of his crimes. When asked by *Playboy* how he, an educated, cultured, presumably moral and upright representative of Germany's best people, could have been a participant in the gruesome Nazi regime, he says the only way he can account for it is the mesmeric powers of Adolph Hitler.

Speer makes it clear that no matter how bad we think Hitler was, he was worse than that. The picture he draws is of a monster completely devoid of any human goodness (Hitler was very kind to his dog, but then so are Mafia chieftans who think nothing of hanging their enemies alive on meathooks, so he doesn't improve his image by liking dogs.).

When I read this article, bringing back all the horrors of concentration camps, cremation ovens, tortures, megalomania which characterized the Nazi regime, it recalled a startling statement made by a distinguished theologian, the late Dr. Nels Ferré. During World War II, when hate for Hitler was a national mania, Ferré preached a sermon in a large, fashionable metropolitan church. In that sermon he said, "I expect to meet Hitler in heaven."

Well, Sir, if You keep an eye on everything as You supposedly do, You will remember what a bruhaha that caused! People just had a fit! They wanted to defrock Ferré, try him for sedition, cut off financial support to the institution where he taught, anything to punish him. The nicest thing anyone said about him was that he was a dirty, Nazi-loving heretic. The epithets were all downhill from that.

Of course, everyone missed the point, or didn't want to get it. Ferré was preaching on the theme of the love of God. He was trying to say that Your love is the strongest force in the universe, and that ultimately nothing can resist it. Since, at the time, Adolph Hitler was about the least godly person anyone knew about, Ferré chose him to make his point. If Hitler is going to be in heaven, who can be excluded?

CHARLES MERRILL SMITH

144

It would be helpful if we knew precisely just how this heaven-hell deal works. You are the final arbiter in who goes where, of course. No one would contest that. But Sir, You have failed to make it entirely clear to us just how You separate the sheep from the goats.

Strict Calvinists, of course, insist that You decide what You decide, and that's that. They say You don't need to abide by any of our ideas of what's right or fair or just or merciful because the fact that You do something makes it right and fair and just and merciful—even condemning a newborn infant to eternal crackling flames.

I reject that. If that is the way it is, then I am Your enemy. On that kind of a system You could take Adolph Hitler into heaven and send Albert Schweitzer to hell, and it would be right and just. Really, Sir, I don't think people, even Calvinists, ought to talk about You that way. Such a preposterous theology means that You are more like Adolph Hitler than You are like Albert Schweitzer. If you are like that, it would mean that You ought to consult a reputable psychiatrist, and we know for a fact that God doesn't have personality problems. Besides, if people got to thinking You are anything like Hitler, it would be very poor public relations. If You are a Calvinist, I could see how You could let Hitler into heaven, but I don't think that You are.

My upbringing has led me to believe that people earn entrance to glory or merit consignment to Hades on the basis of their personal behavior. I have always thought, when I thought about it, that anyone who keeps the Ten Commandments and follows the Sermon on the Mount would make it to paradise. But I can't think of anyone who qualifies. If that is what one has to do, then heaven is a sparsely settled place. You are going to be pretty lonesome. Maybe

You will let us pass if we score 70 percent, like they do in school. But while it may be easy for You to grade us on our behavior, it isn't easy for us. It's only fair, isn't it, that we know our cumulative grade average so if we need more points to pass we can cram a little for the final exam?

Some people say I can get into heaven just by believing the right things. But the batty stuff they say I have to believe, well, I just can't swallow it.

Would You agree with me that heaven and hell are somewhat outmoded concepts?

Whenever I say this, some of my Christian friends come back with the accusation that I have a squishy, sentimental concept of God, that after all, if You are You it is necessary for You to crack down every now and then. Besides, they say, why worry about being good if You let us get away with being bad?

I am not convinced. It seems to me that striving for heaven, or trying to stay out of hell, diverts our attention from the real point of our existence. (Most people are more interested in staying out of hell than they are of getting to heaven, of course. Do You recall the incident when some of his friends found W. C. Fields reading the Bible? Knowing he was not a devout man, they were surprised. "What are you doing?" they asked. "Looking for loopholes," Fields replied.)

Anyway, I see the point of our existence summed up in Jesus' statement that he came that we might have the abundant life. And he wasn't talking about some misty hereafter, either. He meant right now. I'm sure of that. The focus of our efforts, then, should be on achieving the abundant life here, not hereafter.

CHARLES MERRILL SMITH

146

Personally, I go along with Dr. Ferré, please rest his kindly, loving soul. I am willing to leave my eternal destiny in Your hands. I am not willing to trade my chance for an abundant life here by doggedly subscribing to some supposed rules of Yours in order to win the right to a perpetual blast in paradise. I don't know how You are going to do it, but I believe Your love is so strong that somewhere, somehow it will win over the worst sinner the world has ever known.

So, like Dr. Ferré, I expect to meet Hitler in heaven. But I can't be sure of living abundantly, every day, here. I'm going to concentrate on it, though.

32

Save Me from Bitterness

Loving Spirit, Sir . . . I don't have any trouble with envy. For some reason I have no capacity to be put out by the success of others. Maybe I flirt a little with gluttony, not so much with oversize helpings but a certain finickiness with the quality of what I eat. I spurt unchristian tempers now and then, but I have anger pretty well under control.

Before I begin sounding like a self-conscious goody twoshoes let me hasten to confess, Sir, that I have plenty of spiritual failings. The one that bugs me the most is that when I am treated with what I regard as injustice I react with bitterness.

For example, there is this big institution that I served, and served well for many years. It advertises itself as benevolent; it talks a lot about the sacredness of the individual; it collects piles of money for the purpose of helping people. Well, Sir,

148

I won't go into the gory details, but it treated me like a thing. I resented it, I still resent it, and I have to do battle with my bitterness toward it all the time.

Now I don't like bitter people. I try to avoid their company. Bitterness, it seems to me, is among the least lovely of human feelings. It is, I suspect, a form of self-pity, which is a form of spiritual pride—and I know full well how You feel about spiritual pride because the Bible makes it plain that spiritual pride is the big daddy of all sin.

But I can't lick it. At least I haven't yet. The irony is that by treating me in what I consider an unjust manner, the institution forced me to take action which has resulted in my being much happier with life than I was before—except for the bitterness.

You don't need to tell me, Sir, that I am not the only one who has ever been shafted by an institution he has served well. I have a good friend who was thrown out of an institution because he was doing too good a job. His own competence was showing up the incompetence of the top brass. I have counseled countless men who got poured down the drain for no better reason than that the boss needed the job for a moron brother-in-law, or that the executive vice-president's wife didn't like his haircut. I always counseled against bitterness.

But I find I don't take my own advice very well. I need help, and I don't like the feeling that I need help.

Could you pass a miracle and wipe out my tendency to bitterness? I'm tired of the battle.

Or is my salvation tied up with my willingness to continue

the battle? Is this one that I have to solve for myself? I'd prefer that You do it for me, but I'll hang in there if You say I have to.

And I expect that You will say I have to.

CHARLES MERRILL SMITH

33

Would Jesus Drive a Cadillac?

Source of Our Values, Sir . . . Once I was talking with a
Methodist bishop and he related that a friend of his—a prosperous clergyman—was wrestling with the question, "Would
Jesus drive a Cadillac?" He was, of course, trying to ease
his puritan conscience prior to purchasing a Cadillac for
himself.

I turned the question back on the bishop. Would Jesus drive
a Cadillac? The bishop replied that he wasn't sure that
Jesus would drive a Cadillac, but that he sure would if he
could afford it.

Well, I can see that a Methodist bishop might reasonably
drive a Cadillac, because there is the dignity and impres-
siveness of his office to uphold, and not many things are
more dignified and impressive than a Cadillac except maybe

a Rolls Royce, and a Rolls Royce would be a bit much even for a Methodist bishop.

What I am getting at is this, Sir: Is there an authentic Christian life-style, and are there life-styles not permitted a Christian, and where do we draw the line?

This is a question that continually fascinates me. Maybe I'm fascinated by it because my Christian upbringing was weighted toward identifying the Christian faith with an appropriate life-style, or what my particular corner of Protestant Christian culture considered an appropriate life-style.

Nobody laid it out, bound and indexed, and said this is the authentic Christian life-style. We got at it, like the good bishop and his clerical friend, by debating what is permissible to a Christian.

We accepted the Ten Commandments as basic, of course, and nobody questioned them. Nobody even saw any inconsistency between the commandment "Thou shalt not kill" and killing in wars, or executing criminals, or—when the occasion demanded—lynching a few blacks under a banner with the cross of Christ on it.

But what the bishop and his friend were trying to do was test the limits of authentic Christian life-style. They were in that gray area where the Bible doesn't guide us specifically. The Bible doesn't say a Christian can drive a Cadillac. On the other hand, it doesn't say that he can't. An awfully lot of the stuff which makes up our daily lives is in that gray area. Not prohibited. Not approved.

So, "Can a Christian drive a Cadillac?" sounds like a frivolous question, but it isn't.

CHARLES MERRILL SMITH

If I am a serious Christian, how much luxury and opulent living am I permitted to enjoy? Is the most deluxe model of Chevrolet allowable within the limits of Christian life-style, but a Cadillac—which is only a little larger and slightly plushier than the Chevy—off limits? Is the Chevrolet basic transportation and the Cadillac prideful ostentation?

How well is a Christian permitted to dress? Is a business suit from Hart, Schaffner, and Marx Christian (no joke intended) and a nifty number from the Pierre Cardin boutique sinful? Or am I a better disciple of Christ if I buy everything off plain pipe racks? Can a Christian lady wear mink? Is central air conditioning safely inside Christian life-style limits but a home swimming pool going too far toward pagan splendor?

It seems to me, Sir, that a man's life-style is a surface reflection of what he really believes. That's why it's important to decide what is and what is not permissible to the Christian.

If our prosperous clergyman breaks down and buys that Cadillac, drives up to the church in it, and preaches a sermon on the text "Sell all that you have and give it to the poor," am I not likely to think that this joker is putting me on? On the other hand, if he shows me that the Caddy costs him less to drive and own than any other vehicle which transports him in reasonable comfort and safety (Some people claim this is so, especially Cadillac salesmen.), then he has made a very Christian decision.

We would, as Christians, have to find the authority for our life-style in Jesus, wouldn't we? But how?

One way would be to imitate Jesus' life-style as closely as possible. Some people do this. The hippie types who don't go to a barber and live in communes and go around preaching peace and love and share everything with their fellows probably come closest of anyone to imitating Jesus' life-style. Yet, oddly enough, nothing infuriates standard brand middle-class Christians so much as the sight of an unshorn hippie. They love the Sunday school pictures of Jesus with his long tresses and beard, but they get apoplectic if their sons look like those pictures.

Jesus, however, never said we had to imitate his life-style. It isn't forbidden to Christians, but it isn't commanded. And there is good evidence that Jesus accepted as followers people who practiced a very different kind of life-style.

Should we then seek to derive our life-style from the teachings of Jesus?

Is "Sell all you have and give it to the poor" a universal mandate on Christians? If it is, we would depopulate the churches pretty fast. Bible scholars have wiggled out of this one, though, by pointing out that Jesus was addressing himself to a particular person with a particular need when he said this, therefore it doesn't apply to everyone. I expect that they are right.

I have observed that what many Christians do is to fashion their personal tastes and habits into a life-style and then call it Christian. Unchristian life-style then becomes what other people do that I don't care to do.

For example, when I was a boy attending a small Christian college (which one of my irreverent friends said was for "small Christians," a rather snide description, I'm afraid) people argued all the time if a Christian could dance and play cards and go to Sunday baseball games and still be

CHARLES MERRILL SMITH

a Christian. It all seems rather quaint now, but we thought these were serious questions.

Well, I can't dance, and I don't enjoy cards, so it is all right with me if people who dance and play cards are officially dechristianized. But attending a baseball game on Sunday is another thing entirely. I am a baseball fan, and if Baltimore and Boston, or San Francisco and St. Louis are playing on a Sunday and I can get there, I see nothing unchristian about going. People who say I shouldn't are meddling with my freedom of choice.

Thus, the temperance advocate says the alcohol-free life is the only Christian life. But the Christian who likes a nip points out that Jesus drank wine as he smacks his lips over his dry Manhattan. I know people who believe that no Christian woman should use cosmetics, but none of them are Christian drug store owners. Christian drug store owners find nothing unchristian whatever in the liberal use of the creams and goo and paints and powders which are such a high-markup item in their establishments.

For that matter, does an authentic Christian life-style include showing up for the formal worship service of your church every Sunday, or are their alternative ways of practicing your faith which are just as legitimate? Can a Christian smoke tobacco without losing his standing (as all Christians in tobacco-growing states believe), but if he smokes marijuana should he be cast out of the fellowship?

I hate to be critical of You, Sir, but I fear You haven't given us as much help on the question of authentic Christian life-style as You might have given. You haven't spelled it out in the Bible, except for some very general commandments that don't cover many of the day-to-day problems we must solve, and which we try to solve in the light of our faith.

Or is this the way You intended it to be?

P.S. I have decided that Jesus would probably drive a Volkswagen. It is modest in cost. The company doesn't waste money on annual style changes. Rich people often drive them, so even a Methodist bishop could drive one without damage to his prestige. And besides, they have very clever and entertaining ads on TV. I don't own one, but I'm thinking about it.

CHARLES MERRILL SMITH

156

34

Do You Blame Me for Quitting the Ministry?

Sir . . . Let me ask You a question. Do You like preachers better than other people?

Theoretically Your answer has to be no. But I was raised to believe that Your answer is yes. As You no doubt recall, I came from a line of parsonage families. My life revolved around the church. No one ever said to me that ministers occupy a special place in Your affection, but the whole tone and impact of my Protestant Christian culture led me to believe that a Protestant Christian pastor, especially a Methodist Protestant Christian pastor, is a member of a spiritual elite. I have often wondered how large a part this idea played in my choice of profession.

I remember so well the rejoicing in the local congregation when one of its boys was "called to the ministry." The rich people in the congregation hoped that their sons wouldn't hear the call and would opt for more lucrative and socially acceptable vocations such as law or medicine or business. But they too rejoiced when the sons of less affluent members heard the call. A pastor whose church produced a regular batch of prospective preachers had a good claim to promotion to a larger church. Our church camps put the pressure on us to make a decision for "full-time Christian service."

So it wouldn't be surprising if my decision was influenced no little by all this. I expect the greatest influence was my admiration for my father, who was a pastor. But the other had something to do with it.

Well, as You know, Sir, I was a parish pastor for many years, then quit when I was fifty—fifteen years short of the accepted age of retirement. So do You look on my early dropout as a kind of spiritual treason? Have I thrown in the towel on the world's most sacred calling? Do You hold it against me?

I could plead ill health, and then You couldn't hold it against me. After all, I was pastor of this big church, and I developed hypertension, and my blood pressure kept climbing. The doctor said I would probably be O.K. if I took it easier, so I resigned.

But I would be conning You if I claimed that ill health was the real reason I quit, and no one ought to try a con game on God.

When I had time to reflect on my rather abrupt resignation from the pastorate, I realized that the important question was why my blood pressure went up. I finally had to admit to myself that it was from frustration with my job, com-

CHARLES MERRILL SMITH

pounded by a sense of futility, a growing conviction that what I was doing wasn't very important any more. When a fellow feels this way, the only honest thing to do is quit.

Maybe if I could have convinced myself that the ministry was just another job like selling insurance, I would have come to terms with myself. But that old idea that it is the most sacred of professions had infected me more seriously than I had realized. I just couldn't pretend that I was doing Your special work when I didn't believe that I was.

Perhaps if I explain how I feel about dropping out it will mitigate somewhat Your harsh attitude toward me, if, in fact, You do hold a harsh attitude toward me.

I must confess that, from the very beginning, I had some emotional problems with the pastoral ministry.

Some Christian laymen, as You probably know from experience with them, are pretty hard to take. There is a church boss in every congregation, frequently several, who push the preacher around. I do not respond in the ideal Christian manner to being pushed around. I know all about turning the other cheek, and how a soft answer turneth away wrath. But if You eventually admit me to heaven You will have to overlook my low marks in cheek-turning and soft answers.

My clerical superiors were a mixed bag. Some of them were just great, while others were—well, Sir, if You had a bishop who lectured his men all the time on how to spend every minute of the day (he even specified the times we should go to the bathroom, honest), and who considered the highest compliment he had ever received was from a layman who told him he should have gone into business instead of wasting his talents in the ministry because he was such a fine administrator, You wouldn't like it either.

I don't know whether You ever look in on church meetings, conferences, retreats, etc. or not. If You do You can hardly fail to agree with me that they are deadly boring. The Methodists have lots of meetings, and one can't dodge all of them, although my record of absenteeism and late-arrival-early-departure-style attendance was rather spectacular. John Wesley, the founder of Methodism, kept harping on the theme that to waste time is a sin, so I thought I was only avoiding sin when I didn't go, or at least didn't stay long.

But these are trifling complaints. Any employee of a big business corporation has to put up with all this and more.

On the other hand, there was a very great deal about the job of parish pastor I found emotionally satisfying, and a man needs to find emotional satisfaction in his job or it isn't any good.

I got a kick out of building new plants, breathing life into moribund congregations, preaching, teaching, being a community leader. These are all most nourishing to the ego.

I've mentioned to You previously that the genuine pastoral care I was able to give people is still a precious memory. It may sound ghoulish, but—on reflection—I believe that I was most aware of my pastoral contribution at funerals. I found that I could be of spiritual help to people at the time of the death of a loved one perhaps more than at any other time. I didn't exactly enjoy the role, and sometimes cringed from it, but I have the satisfaction of knowing I helped.

So what happened to me?

Who can honestly assess his own motives? Only to You are all hearts open, all desires known. All I can say is that so

CHARLES MERRILL SMITH

long as I never questioned the church's claim that it represented the Kingdom of God on earth I never contemplated quitting its employ. So long as I was convinced it was doing something that desperately needed doing there was a sense of dignity and worth in my job.

But I did question, and I am no longer convinced. When I finally faced the fact that congregations desire a smooth, growing, successful organization above all else, then I had to admit that I, as pastor, was more like the manager of a private club than anything else I could think of. There is nothing terrible about being the manager of a private club, of course. When you are the manager of a big, affluent private club (as I was), the compensation is excellent and the fringe benefits are fantastic. It is a good job, a pleasant life.

But it isn't the Christian ministry, or at least I don't think that it is.

Another facet of my emotional problem with my vocation was that I saw a need for an entirely new kind of pastoral leadership if the church is to meet the challenge of the new age, and I was—by training, experience, taste, and disposition—the old kind of pastoral leader.

I can preach sharp, biblically sound, intellectually respectable sermons—but who wants to listen any more? The new pastoral leadership needs to know its way around in new techniques of communication. I don't know my way around in the new techniques.

I am knowledgeable in the field of classical Christian worship and can put that kind of service together as well as anyone. But that doesn't turn anyone on anymore. What's wanted, and needed, is new modes of worship to fit the day, and I'm no good at that because I'm still on the old wavelength.

As I said in a previous conversation, I believe the church has to make radical changes if it is to live. I hope it does. But I'm not equipped to be a new-style leader, and I don't intend to insist that it ought to go on doing what it has been doing because I am only equipped to give old-style leadership. Too many preachers are doing that already, from Pope Paul on down, Catholic and Protestant, and, I suppose, Jewish.

Another little point I would like to make in my own favor is that I was a pastor for nearly three decades. Is thirty years at one job maybe enough? Kurt Vonnegut insists that twenty years is the longest anyone ought to stick to doing the same thing, and he's regarded as a pretty smart man.

Anyone who stays with the same job for a long period of time is bound to suffer battle fatigue. Toward the end I noticed the signs in myself.

I was no longer quick to confront situations that I knew from experience needed confrontation. I would try to avoid the decisive moment and hope it would go away. I grew weary too quickly of good people who insisted on bad policies in the church thinking they were good policies. Finally, I couldn't face fifteen more years of doing the same old thing.

I notice this happening to people in other professions. There seems to be a rash of dropoutitis among corporation executives, teachers, lawyers, successful men in various occupations. It seems to hit in early middle age. Maybe that should tell me something about myself.

As You know, Sir, because I have talked to You privately

CHARLES MERRILL SMITH

162

about it a number of times, I suffered some withdrawal pains.

One trouble with my profession is that one's professional identity becomes so bound up and interwoven with his identity as a person. I found I didn't know where the clerical identity left off and my personal identity began.

This, I think, is one of the bad side effects of ordination. We come to look on ourselves as very special, not because of any virtue in ourselves but through the conferred virtue by the laying on of hands. Since it is much easier to structure our self-image with the conferred virtue than it is to struggle toward personhood, that is what most of us do. Then, when the conferred virtue is stripped away, we don't know where to look for ourselves. This I believe to be spiritually unhealthy. We are a person first, and a professional man second. This order should not be reversed.

On the other hand, I have found real spiritual renewal in starting another career in middle age.

It is a little scary. There is no security in it. I'm making about half as much as my last annual salary from the church I was serving. But there is a sense of freedom. I'm having fun at my work once again. I don't say that what I am doing now is more important than what I was doing, but it is no less important. And I have this wonderful feeling that I am learning a new vocation, that the future has exciting possibilities for me which it didn't have before.

It may not work out that way, of course. Things may go badly. The exciting possibilities may be illusions. But, Sir, I had to try. I hope You understand that. No way of life is any good when it has lost its meaning. A fellow is just a time-server under those conditions. And I couldn't stand being a time-server pretending I was serving You.

As I have stated, I'm still a card-carrying clergyman. I'm just a minister without portfolio, if You will forgive a bad pun. I can even conceive of conditions under which I could find meaning and spiritual exhilaration in the pastoral ministry, but I do not believe they will occur in my lifetime, so it is highly unlikely that I will reenter that particular branch of Your service.

So, in the light of what I am hoping You will accept as a strong case for doing what I did, perhaps You won't hold it against me that I dropped out of the pastoral ministry.

And I would be grateful for any help and support You can give me in the future, just as You have in the past.

CHARLES MERRILL SMITH

35

Do I Need Heroes?

You Who Alone Are Perfect, Sir . . . There is this chap named Jim Bouton, a former major league pitcher of some repute, who has written a couple of books about his experiences in baseball. Most books by sports figures are very tame stuff. They portray professional athletics as a godly enterprise, and picture the athletes as clean, pure, noble, and brave. After all, athletes are idols to young Americans (and to a lot of old Americans, also).

But Bouton didn't write it that way. He showed the good and commendable side of these nationally known athletes (where there was a good and commendable side), but he also detailed the mean, the stupid, the ugly aspects of the game and of those who play it.

Well, there was a violent reaction, both from players and

165

fans. No one said Bouton was lying. No one accused him of false reporting. No one questioned the accuracy of what he wrote. Almost everyone, though, complained that he shouldn't have written it. It destroys the image of many heroes, the argument went. Then these critics, dozens of them, asked the question I want to ask You, Sir: "We need heroes, don't we?"

Do we?

The theory is that we grow and develop through imitating someone we admire tremendously. It is easier to pattern ourselves after a person than it is to follow a set of abstract ideals. Because we respond more readily to a person than to a sermon is why, no doubt, You sent Jesus Christ to show us what You want of us.

The catch to the hero business, Sir, is which hero to pick as my model. Excluding Jesus Christ, who is every Christian's supreme hero, whom do I follow? What mortal man, no matter how sublime, should I take as my model?

Most boys pick their fathers as their original hero. I know I did. He was an exceptionally fine father, even discounting a natural prejudice in his favor I'm bound to have.

But what if he had been a bad father, an evil man? Quite a few fathers are persons no one ought to imitate. Personally, I am very glad that Jesus told us to think of You as a father, because I had a good father. But what about the kid who has a mean, no-good old man? Or who has no father at all?

Another drawback to imitating a person or persons whom you admire is that we more often than not pick the wrong kind of persons. We confuse publicity with moral and spiritual worth. Whenever they take a poll of the most admired

CHARLES MERRILL SMITH

166

men and women, the winners are always presidents and movie stars. This is admiring someone for who he is rather than what he is, a dangerous method for picking heroes.

Then, there is the danger illustrated by Bouton's books.

If people idolize Mickey Mantle for his clean-cut look, splendid physique, tremendous athletic skill, and courage and determination in the face of suffering, they are reacting normally to a heroic figure.

But when they read that he was sometimes mean to little kids, spent much time in bars, and tended to maudlin self-pity, does he become a bum? Should we be spared the dark side of the truth about Mantle so that we may hold to Mantle the hero? Are news writers and public relations departments doing us a service when they conspire to conceal the less savory facts about an admired public figure?

Sir, I firmly believe that personal growth, becoming a better person, is tied up with imitating people who have achieved personal worth.

Although I haven't succeeded in imitating him noticeably in my own life, one of my heroes is Albert Schweitzer. To me, as to most of the world, he typifies much of what is genuinely good in the human spirit. His breadth of compassion for the suffering, his willingness to sacrifice himself for the sake of others, his passion to serve, all have about them, Sir, a Christlike quality. He appeared to be "the man for others," to use Bonhoeffer's description of Jesus.

One of the remembered experiences which will never leave me was, many years ago, hearing Schweitzer speak. This imperial-looking old man had a presence hard to describe.

HOW TO TALK TO GOD . . .

It was a compound of authority and gentleness. Many people have one or the other, but seldom both. I imagine that Christ had it. Schweitzer is a pretty good sort of hero for anyone. Scholar, master musician, noted theologian, medical doctor, humanitarian—he was all of these. What a marvelous combination!

Does it diminish him then, Sir, that—so we are told—he was often irascible, resistant to innovation, and apparently a failure as a husband? (I am inclined to sympathize with his wife, who finally gave up and lived mostly apart from him for many years, because saints are notoriously difficult to live with.) I do not like irascible people, and rigid opposition to innovation strikes me as stupid. Should I then cast Dr. Schweitzer from my hall of heroes?

To put it in a capsule, I have been around long enough to know that any hero I might pick will have, if not clay feet, at least some qualities I wish he didn't have. There must be a flaw even in Ralph Nader, although neither General Motors' detectives nor I have been able to uncover it.

Since I believe I need heroes I have a problem. I want to see the embodiment of courage, zeal, kindliness, justice, service, joy, humor, idealism, love, mercy, tolerance, good will, and all the other traits, values, and attitudes which make up the best in human personality. I want to see them not in a book or a moral treatise, but up and walking around on two feet. I want to see them in people whose example will inspire me to go and do likewise.

So what I do, Sir, is to expect the imperfections. I know they are there, even if I do not immediately apprehend them. After all, the Bible tells me to expect imperfection even in the best of humans, so I'm not being a cynic.

CHARLES MERRILL SMITH

Then I ignore the flaws and admire the virtues. By assembling the virtues from, say, a dozen heroes I have a pretty good composite of what the Christian personality ought to be.

It is, I admit, a little like cheating at solitaire, but—like cheating at solitaire—it works. The method permits me to view the Christian characteristics in action, thus helping me to grow morally and spiritually, and that's what heroes are for.

Do You have any fault to find with my system for employing heroes?

36

Do You Feel Sorry for the Trapped?

Ever-Compassionate Sir . . . The world is so full of enormous suffering that sometimes I can hardly bear to think about it. What with television coverage we are made instantly aware of the horrible consequences of a tidal wave in Pakistan or an earthquake in the Andes or starvation in Biafra. Anyone almost is heartbroken at the first sight of this elemental human misery. I have never quite been able to square all this human suffering with Your love for us all and Your omnipotence. I know that a lot of smart theologians have given us ingenious explanations of what they call the problem of evil, but all the answers have gaps in them. I want to take it up with You sometime, but not right now.

Maybe, in the light of all this elemental suffering, it is foolish to spare any sorrow for a less dramatic class of sufferers. I am referring to those millions of people who have plenty

170

to eat and wear, and perhaps possess a respectable bank account, but are trapped by some circumstance of life—and they know it.

One common trap is a fellow's job.

It is nothing less than spiritually excruciating to be tied to a job which at best is a dull, meaningless task and at worst something you actively hate.

I know too many people who are in this particular trap. What they once thought they wanted to do they don't want to do any more. Or they took a job because it was available, and then a quarter of a century later they wake up and realize they are thinking about retirement. All that time has gone, and they haven't done anything they really wanted to do with it. Now, with the home for senior citizens just around the corner and the cemetery over the hill, they know they will never do these things they once hoped to do. It isn't easy to live with hopes never realized or dreams never tried.

But they are shut in. Mortgages, a level of life-style, family considerations, lack of options, fear of insecurity, these and so many more circumstances slam the cell door. No breakout is possible for them. They are trapped.

I expect, if we could ever amass the statistics, we would find that more women than men feel trapped.

Women, it seems to me, are trapped by too much to do when their children are growing up, and not enough to do when the family is raised. My observation is that this is particularly hard on educated, intelligent women who are smart enough to realize that washing diapers and making formula as well as bridge clubs and playing at charity underemploy her need to be a person as well as a wife.

Both men and women, of course, suffer from being trapped in mediocre or downright bad marriages.

Perhaps they can't separate because of strongly held opposition to divorce. Or they put up with the situation for the sake of the children. Or they hope it will get better. Or they are constitutionally unable to admit failure. They are trapped.

I'm not blaming You, Sir, but it hardly seems fair that life lays so many snares for the unwary.

Pity the fellow who realizes, in midlife, that he will never live up to his potential because of an inadequate education. He is trapped.

How horrible it must be when a man's livelihood depends upon pleasing a gross, ignorant, and overbearing boss. That is a bad trap.

How unpleasant must be the life of a sensitive, romantically inclined woman whose husband treats sex like a belch—a necessary physical release. Trap is the word for her situation.

I have known many boys who were trapped by their fathers' ambition for them. The boys might want to be mechanics, or sailors, or flute players, or race drivers. But because of paternal pressure they struggled with law school, or entered business, or became dentists.

I have known girls who were trapped by peer group conformity or the desire to be accepted into premature and undesired sexual experience. That kind of trap leaves permanent scars on the spirit.

We could take the attitude, "Well, they don't need to be

trapped. They can break out." Or we could say, "When people are trapped, it's their own fault. They made their own mistakes."

I suppose, Sir, that both are true. But sometimes escape from our traps entails action so severe that our last state would be worse than our first. And mistakes can be perceived quite clearly as we look back, but they aren't so apparent when we are looking forward.

Anyway, the world is full of people who are trapped and who are suffering agonies of the spirit because of it. Do You feel sorry for them? I expect You do, because I do, and You are far more compassionate than I.

So I'm sending up a prayer for all who are now in traps they want to be out of, but can't get out of.

I don't know what You ought to do about it. Help the ones who could get out to see how to do it, maybe. And for the ones who can't get out, Your comfort for the troubled spirit would be in order.

These people need Your help.

37

Is My Restlessness a Blessing or a Disease?

Ever-Serene Spirit, Sir . . . It isn't that I can't stick to anything. You know I stayed with one job for ten years, and with some others for respectable spans of time.

But I get restless. Even when I'm in places I like, I get the itch to move on. In fact, the attacks of restlessness are most severe when I suddenly realize I am becoming quite content with where I am and what I am doing. It's as if my spirit has a horror of ruts, no matter how comfortable they may be.

There are serious logistical disadvantages to being restless. You don't get any roots down. You hesitate to own anything that isn't portable. You get so you hold yourself just a little aloof from any kind of local involvements. It isn't always possible to pick up and go when you feel the urge.

If the celestial lending library has a section for detective fiction, You, Sir, should get one of the Nero Wolfe books. Nero Wolfe, the big fat detective, is a perpetual delight to mystery-story readers, of which there must be many in heaven. Anyway, Nero Wolfe hardly ever leaves his old brownstone house on West 35th Street because he has a theory that where you are going is unlikely to be any improvement over where you already are.

I'm just the opposite. I am ever sanguine about the possibilities somewhere else. Long experience has taught me that sometimes somewhere else is an improvement over where I am and sometimes it isn't. But experience has in no way snuffed out my optimism.

What I can't decide, Sir, is whether my restlessness is a blessing or a disease.

Sometimes I think it to be a disease if I am running away from something, and a blessing if I am running toward something. But usually it is some of both.

No matter where we are, there are always problems, involvements, fouled-up relationships, etc. which it is nice to leave behind us. It may be a cheap way to write off these emotional liabilities, kind of a spiritual year of Jubilo, but it works.

On the other hand, there is a lift, an exhilaration in trying a new place. New scenery, new faces, even new problems tend to be refreshing to me, and to most people I expect. It is fun to run toward something.

I have to curb my restlessness now and then, and I know I should. But would it be healthy to cure it entirely? I don't know.

HOW TO TALK TO GOD . . .

I also have this opposite kind of pull down deep inside me. I have a hazy, ill-delineated vision of a place where I would like to come to rest.

As nearly as I can make it out through the murk of my imagining, it is a large Tudor, or maybe Georgian, house set in a rolling landscape, bracketed by trees, with a river in the back and maybe the sea, or at least a lake, in front. It has tessellated floors, and lots of fireplaces, and ceiling beams, and a tremendous library.

In my imagination I know I would be content in this ultima Thule of mine. But a part of my vision is that, while located in bucolic splendor, the place is not far from a city and an airport. I want to be able to get somewhere else in a hurry if the place palls on me.

So, disease or blessing, I guess my restlessness is incurable. I'll just ask You then, Sir, to guide my journeyings to good places.

CHARLES MERRILL SMITH

176

38

Do You Want Me to Be a Mystic?

Dispenser of All Truth, Sir . . . There is a lady I know who belongs to an informal group of Christian women. These women get together occasionally to hear what You have to say to them. Sometimes they will sit silently around a table, palms up. They say they can feel the power of Your Holy Spirit entering them through their upturned palms.

Now these ladies may be a little far out, but I know scads of Christians who depend on You to speak to them directly. As You know, people who claim to apprehend divine reality by direct reception, unfiltered by the process of reason, are called mystics.

I am well aware that Christian history is studded with sincere, reverent mystics. It is not my intent to question the validity of mystical experience. After all, who am I to judge people such as St. Augustine, Meister Eckhart, Count Zinzendorf, or St. Catherine of Genoa?

What I want to know is, do I have to be one to be counted a good Christian? Or, would I be a better Christian if I were one?

After many years of waiting for that transforming, edifying, ecstatic experience the mystics say I should receive, I have concluded, Sir, that I am just not the mystical type. Perhaps I do not believe strongly enough. Or maybe I have a spiritual gland missing. I have decided that I'll just have to muddle along as best I can without mystical experience.

Sir, there must be millions of nonmystical Christians like me. And I'll bet if You questioned them You would discover that they all feel a bit guilty for not having had a mystical experience. All of us suspect we are missing out on something tremendous, because our more mystically inclined Christian friends tell us that we are.

If it isn't too much trouble, I wish that You would tell all Christian mystics to quit acting as if they pity us nonmystics. Maybe they do pity us, but it would be a Christian virtue if they would learn to conceal it.

At any rate, I hope You don't downgrade us nonmystics. I'm sure we all would be mystics if we could be, but some of us can't. Perhaps the mystical spirit is a gift You give to some and deny to others.

I'll be happy to be denied the gift. I just don't want to be looked on as a second-class Christian because I don't have it.

Some of my mystical friends do look on me as inferior to mystical-type Christians, but I'm betting that You don't.

CHARLES MERRILL SMITH

178

39

Do You Still Work Six Days a Week?

Builder of the Universe, Sir . . . It is recorded in the Book of Genesis that You manufactured the world in six days and then knocked off on the seventh. Your six-day week has more or less established the attitude toward work contained in the Protestant Ethic. Therefore, I have some questions about it.

Were these eight-hour days You put in? Was this a special effort on Your part, or is this how You always do it? Do You get a month's vacation? Genesis doesn't mention any of these details.

What I am really anxious to know is if hard work is a virtue and a necessary part of the process of salvation. I have been brought up to believe that it is both of these. Most Americans are convinced that a man's willingness to work is the measure of his worth as a person. This is why we are so hostile to people on welfare, hippies, and other nonlaboring citizens.

To give You an accurate picture of our American attitude toward hard work, just in case it has escaped Your attention, I have prepared another fable. I call it

THE SQUIRREL WHO KEPT HIS NOSE CLEAN

There was this squirrel named Henry who worked like a dog all the time gathering nuts and things. He lived in the attic of an old house, and it was crammed with nuts because Henry and his family couldn't use them up as fast as Henry gathered them. People would say, "Henry, why do you gather more nuts than you can use? You wouldn't be able to eat all these if you lived to be fifteen or sixteen years old." But Henry would answer, "I find my happiness here as well as the true meaning of life in gathering nuts. If everyone gathered nuts all day as I do, it would be a better world. Besides, it's good for the health. All that burrowing and sniffing around keeps my nose clean."

Just down the block was a coon named Byron. Byron wasn't a bit like Henry. He lived in an abandoned church with a steeple so rotten that birds and bats and who knows what else nested in it. But Byron wouldn't fix it. "Let the birds and the bats live there, what do I care?" he said. "Anyway, it's too much trouble to fix it."

Byron didn't have a job. He spent his days strumming on a zither, reading novels by Gene Genet and Willa Cather, and watching television. He never wore a white shirt and tie, and since he didn't bathe often he didn't smell so good. But he was quite popular, had a party almost every night, and all the lady coons were quite taken with him.

"Disgraceful!" Henry would say whenever he passed Byron's home while on his nut-gathering expeditions.

CHARLES MERRILL SMITH

180

"Why are you wasting a lovely day like this in the old squirrel race?" Byron would reply amiably, which infuriated Henry.

Henry lived an uneventful life, and died full of years and with an attic stuffed with nuts.

Byron, one night, got a little drunk and in his exuberance decided to ring the church bell. But because so many bats had taken up residence in the steeple, the weight was too much for the rotten old bell support, and when Byron pulled the rope, the bell came crashing down, smashing him up something awful. Since he didn't have Blue Cross or Medicare, he spent the rest of his days in a poorhouse, and was buried in a pauper's grave.

MORAL: *It is better to have nuts in the attic than bats in the belfry.*

While the moral of this fable is consonant with the Protestant Ethic and my own training, lately I have been having some doubts about it. Is hard work all that good for me? Is diligent labor the road to salvation? Isn't there a kind of mindlessness to Henry's routine? Is some part of life's meaning to be found outside a person's vocation or job? While Byron would have been better off, no doubt, with a bit of Henry's ethical perspective, wouldn't Henry have benefited greatly if he had adopted some of Byron's outlook?

Or, to put it another way, Henry is more admirable than Byron, but Byron would be a lot more fun to have around than Henry. In all honesty, though I know I shouldn't, I like Byron better than Henry.

Which one do You like better?

40

Will You Forgive Me 490 Prejudices?

Benign Sir . . . Jesus said we are supposed to forgive 70 times 7 offenses, which, if my multiplication is correct, comes to 490 forgivenesses. I assume that You would do no less for me, and I hope this applies to prejudices, because I have at least 490, maybe more—I haven't counted them lately.

Strangely, I try to maintain a self-image of a man who arrives at conclusions without the influence of prejudice. But in my more lucid moments I know I'm kidding myself. Let me give you an example.

The other night one of my favorite TV news programs showed two different groups of demonstrators. One was made up of the radical left. The marchers all wore the standard way-out garb of the movement—dingy jeans, sandals, fringed jackets, that sort of thing. They all had long hair. Most of the men sported beards, Fu Manchu mustaches, and bare chests. Both sexes managed to appear bathless.

The other group was composed of tenants in a luxury apartment protesting landlord negligence. They were quietly arrayed in the the best of taste.

Both groups pleaded their cause to the TV reporter. It struck me at the time how sane and reasonable were the arguments of the upper-middle-class tenants, and how kooky and irrational the crusade of the radicals. But do You know, Sir, when I analyzed the causes, I had to admit that the rich tenants, though perhaps with a genuine grievance, were only engaged in a self-serving technique, while the radicals— whether we agree with them or not—were pursuing a selfless ideal.

What had happened, I realized, was that I had been betrayed by one of my prejudices.

You see, Sir, I instinctively respond favorably to the person who is clean, neat, and well accoutred. I find his thoughts, doctrines, ideas, philosophies more credible than the preachments of the sloppy and ill-kempt.

Let me make it clear that there is much about the New Left's dogma I consider repellent. Not all radical militants advocate violence, but some do, and I don't like their violence any better than the violence of the Ku Klux Klan. Many of the New Left are unduly self-righteous, irrational, and unrealistic. But there is no way for me to dodge the fact that their grooming turns me off, so I would probably be prejudiced against their ideas even if what they advocate is 100 percent good, true, and beautiful.

William Kunstler is never going to make even the last spot on the list of the ten best-dressed men. Eldridge Cleaver may be a leader of sorts, but not in sartorial elegance. Timothy Leary takes many trips, but none of them, apparently, to a first-class tailor. David Dellinger's wardrobe would appall the editors of *Gentlemen's Quarterly*. I don't care for their grooming, so I discount their ideas.

I have mustered what arguments I can to support my prejudice. Doesn't good grooming indicate a necessary self-respect? Is not a carefully arranged costume a sign of a carefully arranged mind? Didn't John Wesley say that cleanliness is next to godliness?

But it won't wash. Mature reflection exposed gaping holes in my prejudice.

If the well-dressed prophet is to carry more weight than the shabby, then Adam Clayton Powell, always dapper, is to be preferred over Martin Luther, who often slept in his clothes. Frank Sinatra would surpass the late Mohandas K. Gandhi as a model of moral conduct.

Although John Wesley was scrupulously clean, one doubts that St. John of the Cross used underarm deodorant. Henry Ward Beecher was something of a dandy, but the late Merton Rice, one of the most persuasive preachers America has produced, wore his black pulpit cutaway coats until they turned green with age.

My gloomy conclusion is that I am the victim of a silly prejudice which has not a shred of evidence in its favor. Evangelists, prophets, philosophers, politicians, anyone preaching a point of view should be judged on the quality of his ideas and not on the quality of his haberdashery.

CHARLES MERRILL SMITH

Some people with whom I am acquainted are convinced that Republicans are more trustworthy than Democrats (and vice versa, of course). I cannot count the times people have tried to convert me to the notion that Negroes are, by nature, inferior to whites. I have several friends who would be unable to accept the idea of a Jew as president of the United States.

I think these are silly, stupid prejudices—but then, they aren't my particular hang-ups. Maybe some of these same people find my preferences for prophets in Brooks Brothers suits a hilariously irrational prejudice, which it is.

I have plenty of other irrational prejudices, too.

I don't like Rose Kennedy, the New York Yankees, or Bill Buckley's columns. The songs which were popular during my high-school years sound infinitely better than the popular music of today. Radio preachers who end their message with an appeal to the listeners, to "help us keep this vital ministry alive" all strike me as charlatans, although I know some of them may well be sincere, devoted men of integrity. Martha Mitchell, Henry Kissinger, and Senator Eastland turn me off. I firmly believe that motorcycles should be outlawed.

I am aware, Sir, that some of my prejudices are rather harmless and do not actually require Your forgiving attention. They won't hurt me much, and probably won't bother anyone else.

But some of them aren't so innocuous. Perhaps I can't be rid of them at a snap of a finger or by making a New Year's resolution, for I know that my emotions usually outrace my wisdom. But I'll try, honest I will.

Meanwhile, to face the fact that my prejudices are prejudices rather than sound and reasoned conclusions is some help. At least, this self-knowledge helps me to laugh at myself when I find myself in the grip of some grotesque theory entirely unsupportable by logic or fact or sweet reason.

I'm counting on this technique to save me from the more malign idiocies to which I, along with the rest of the human race, am vulnerable.

I'm also counting on Your forgiveness.

CHARLES MERRILL SMITH

186

41

I Still Believe You Inspired the King James Version

Source of All Knowledge, Sir . . . During my senior year in college I was a student pastor to a couple of small churches, as You may remember. One of my duties was to conduct a midweek prayer service, which You were supposed to attend, of course, but which I suspect You skipped once in awhile because there was a dreary monotony to the prayers uttered there. I mean, when You had heard one of them You had heard all of them, and busy as You are it would be unreasonable to insist that You attend every session.

Anyway, at this service I mentioned that I was studying Greek so as to better understand the New Testament. A pious, unpleasant old lady (what Mark Twain called a "good woman in the worst sense of the word") criticized my Greek studies as unchristian. Her argument was that Jesus and St. Paul spoke English as recorded in the King James Version of the Scriptures, and that I should stick to the original biblical language.

Well, Sir, not many people believe that the New Testament was written in English, but thousands, maybe millions, of Christians are convinced that You dictated the King James Version of the Bible. One mark of a stalwart faith in some Christian circles is the rejection of any translation of the Bible except the KJV.

I think it only fair to warn anyone who believes this not to read *The Learned Men* by Gustavus Paine. It tells the story, fascinating to me but no doubt disturbing to many, of how the King James Version came into being, and of the men responsible for it.

On January 16, 1604 (a Monday), Dr. John Rainolds, president of Corpus Christi College, Oxford, said to King James I: "May your majesty be pleased to direct that the Bible be now translated, such versions as are now extant not answering to the original."

Dr. Rainolds, who must have earned a privileged place in paradise for this suggestion, was a Puritan clergyman and reputed to be one of the most learned men in England. The king responded to Rainold's request by stating that he didn't think much of any of the English translations (which included the Coverdale Bible, known as the "Bugs Bible" because it read Psalm 91:5 "thou shalt not be afraide of any bugges by night," and the Geneva Bible, known as "the Breeches Bible" because it translated Genesis 3:7 "and they sewed fig leaves together, and made themselves breeches"). It is as obvious to us as it was to King James that a new translation was needed, because anyone knows You talk better than that. King James went on to add that the Geneva Bible was the worse, but his gripe against it was not so much the language as that it did not uphold the divine right of kings as he thought it should. King James was very partial to the doctrine of the divine right of kings.

The king, who was one of the great royal procrastinators of history, finally got around to appointing fifty-four "learned men" to translate the new version. If, Sir, as the King James Version buffs claim, You picked the translators and told them what to write, You surely chose some odd characters to do Your work.

Dr. Rainolds, of course, was the very model of a brilliant, pious, circumspect Christian. But some of the others—oh, my!

Edward Lively, professor of Hebrew at Cambridge, was a pretty straight guy I suppose, although he was always broke and hiding from his creditors. Since he had thirteen children, perhaps we should overlook this.

Most people would approve Your choice of Dean Lancelot Andrewes of Westminster. After all, he had a command of fifteen languages, which is a lot of languages even for a scholar. We still use his written prayers as devotional aids, and nearly everyone finds them inspiring. Also, Andrewes had many personal qualities which I, at least, associate with the Christian personality. He was gentle, amiable, and pleasant to have around. He was a high churchman, although that is neither here nor there, as one can be a good Christian high churchman or a good Christian low churchman. I doubt if it makes any difference to You.

Andrewes, however, was a leader in demanding that Bartholomew Legate, a sort of early day Unitarian, be burned at the stake for heresy, which the king finally did on March 18, 1611. Even if we allow for a different cultural climate in the seventeenth century, I find it hard to condone Christians' burning people at the stake, no matter if the culprits have committed the heinous sin of denying the Trinity. I hope You soaked Andrewes in purgatory for a long sentence before admitting him to heaven.

I probably wouldn't have chosen Dr. Hadrian Saravia as one of the translators if it had been up to me. He was the oldest of the translators, which is O.K., and he was foreign born, which is also O.K. But, as one of his colleagues said, he was "a terrible high churchman." My experience with terrible high churchmen is that they want everything in the Bible to mean that everyone should be terrible high churchmen. I would suspect Dr. Saravia's objectivity, but maybe You knew something about him that I don't.

I agree with You in the choice of John Layfield. He had made a voyage to the West Indies as chaplain to the Earl of Cumberland, and a man who has had some experience of the world is bound to be less parochial in his views than people who have never been anywhere. Also, he had an earthy, repertorial literary style, which no doubt helped to modify the lofty, scholarly tone of his learned co-workers. Scholars tend to write in a fashion calculated to win the admiration of other scholars, which is a way of saying that they can muck up the best of thoughts and ideas. I'm sure this causes much pain in heaven, especially when the latest batch of books on theology arrives. This is why, I suppose, You saw to it that a guy like Layfield was one of the translators of the KJV.

I don't understand, however, why You selected Richard "Dutch" Thompson to be one of the translators. Even though

CHARLES MERRILL SMITH

190

he was rector of Snailwell, Cambridgeshire, an acquaintance said of him that he was "a debauched drunken English Dutchman who seldom went to bed one night sober." Could the laymen in his parish at Snailwell have been that bad? I admit that though he got plastered in the parsonage every night, he could handle his booze, and that he got up every morning able to get on competently with his translating duties—but I still wonder why You picked him. I suppose You had Your reasons.

I do approve, however, of Your choice of Miles Smith. It seems to me that You demonstrated surpassing good judgment in naming him the general editor for the KJV. Scholars say that there is more of Miles Smith in the King James translation than of any other one man, so he must have been pretty good.

There are some items I can't square, though, with the cherished doctrine of the verbal inspiration of the Scriptures, if Mr. Paine's account is to be believed, and I'm sure it is.

If You were dictating it, word by word as the doctrine holds, then why did it take fifty-four guys six years to do the job? The Bible isn't all that big. Fifty-four competent secretaries could handle it in a few days.

Also, if You sent the information direct, why did the translators quarrel among themselves constantly over what to put down, as Mr. Paine tells us they did?

And if these fifty-four translators were taking dictation from You, how come they never got paid for it? No one has ever accused You of being cheap. Your more successful servants today, such as popular evangelists and pastors of multi-thousand-member churches are all in the bucks. Even if they had just been splitting royalties back then, George Abbot, who lived to be 103, and Andrew Bing, who outlived all the other translators, would have died rich. As a working author, I feel that the denial of royalties to the translators of the KJV could have set a very bad precedent.

Mr. Paine tells us, though, that being a translator did help a man's career in the church. Many of them became bishops, which I suppose is reward enough in this life for any man. I think it's a gas that the Puritan clergymen among the translators, who were bitterly opposed on principle to anyone being a bishop, modified their attitude when they were actually offered bishoprics. At least they all accepted the office. Maybe they didn't want to insult the king by refusing.

Another thing—if You instituted and ran the King James project, why did You arrange it so that King James I got the credit? He was a rotten king, even as kings go, and the standard for kings is one of the more modest standards by which people are measured. James I would have disappeared in the dust of history, mercifully forgotten, except that his name is attached to the King James Version of the Scriptures.

So people who want to believe in the doctrine of the verbal inspiration of the Scriptures had better not read *The Learned Men*. The book makes it plain that the translation was the work of fallible human beings.

However, I still believe You had a big hand in it. Not because it is the most accurate translation of the Bible. It isn't. Not because it is the most illuminating and informative translation. The Revised Standard Version beats it forty ways from Sunday on those counts.

CHARLES MERRILL SMITH

I believe the King James Version was divinely inspired because these learned men produced one of history's true works of art. The late H. L. Mencken, a professed and militant atheist, said it best.

"It is," he said, "probably the most beautiful piece of writing in all the literature of the world."

I am convinced, Sir, that anything so beautiful as the King James Version of the Scriptures had to be divinely inspired. I am grateful to You for it.

42

Am I Really a Jew, and Is That O.K. with You?

Ecumenical Spirit, Sir . . . A couple of days ago I was a member of a dinner party, and the lady on my left (a real dazzler, I should report, both in appearance and personality) started asking me questions about my theological opinions. It turned out that she had plenty of questions about the theological views her Sunday school teacher, her pastor, and her fellow church members kept telling her she ought to hold—but that's another story.

So after some conversation, she said to me, "What's the difference between what you believe and what a Jew believes?"

You know, Sir, she made me search my own mind and heart for an answer. I could have given her a snow job, a lot of double-talk about the theological distinction between Juda-

194

ism and Christianity, the kind of stuff the Christian pros put out when they are trying to sell people on the superiority of their brand. But she would have seen through that, she deserved better, and anyway I wasn't inclined to hand out the official orthodox party line—although I have done it at times, for which I hope You have forgiven me.

So I said to her, "I guess there really isn't much difference between what a conservative or a reformed Jew believes and what I believe."

Sir, I confess to a mild shock when forced to admit my theological kinship with Judaism. Not that I am anti-Semitic. Whatever my sins may be, I'm not a victim of that kind of nonsense. It's that I have always assumed that a Christian is distinctively different from disciples of any other religion. But I am one with the Jew in affirming the goodness of Your creation. I believe in the values of justice and mercy and kindness as does the Jew. I believe that the ultimate destiny of history is in Your hands, and so does my Hebrew brother. I believe that each day should be greeted joyously and lived fully, as Jesus taught his disciples, and as the Jew believes.

This delightful lady who raised the question was too tactful to sock it to me on the doctrine of the atonement, or more accurately, doctrines of the atonement. However, I expect that a lot of Christians would say a Jew doesn't believe in the atoning sacrifice of Jesus Christ, and Christians do. My answer to that is that no one can pin the label of heretic on me over the atonement, because there has never been an official, orthodox, certified doctrine of the atonement. Various sects have adopted different versions of the atonement as orthodox for their groups, but no church council ever pronounced on it.

On reflection, I decided that I would differ from a conservative or reformed Jew in the emphasis I put on Jesus Christ in my life.

The Jew (excluding the orthodox Jew, of course) would say that Jesus was a great teacher and should be honored as such. I say he is more than that. I do more than revere his teachings and derive guidance from his example. I can't explain it exactly, Sir, because it is impossible to be precise about ultimate things. It is the totality of Jesus—teaching, life, relationships, priorities, which add up to a total larger than the sum of the parts. My Jewish friends wouldn't buy this.

But I have to admit that there isn't much difference between us. I'd get along fine at the synagogue if I'd learn a little Hebrew. So maybe I'm a Jew at heart.

Is this O.K. with You?

After all, Jesus and the disciples were all Jews, so I'll be in good company in heaven.

CHARLES MERRILL SMITH

196

43

Should I Leave a Tract with the Tip?

Hound of Heaven, Sir . . . I'm sure You understand that I'm not calling You a dog, but only using Francis Thompson's title of the lovely poem he wrote about You always seeking, always pursuing us to help us get squared away to life. His poem pictures You as a gentle, loving, but relentless cosmic evangelist. I don't make it sound so great, but Thompson does. To me, it is one of the most appealing pictures of what You are like ever penned. Of course, that's what poets are for, to say great things in a beautiful and compelling form.

What reminded me of this was an incident at the dinner party I mentioned in my last communication. Our host, a bright and sophisticated Christian layman, was paying the check, and his wife said, "When we were in college and went out to dinner, he always left a tract with the tip." In other words, he was very pious back then, and never missed a chance to do a little evangelistic work. But he doesn't leave a religious tract with the tip anymore.

Now if You think it is important to seek us to save us, it would follow logically that we ought to be doing what we can to seek and save people too. Is this fellow, sincere Christian that he is, not so good a Christian now as he was in the days when he left a tract with the tip?

I don't know how You feel about it, Sir, but I think You should overlook his failure to leave a wake of religious tracts behind him anymore. I didn't ask him why he has ceased the habit, but the reasons aren't hard to guess.

For one thing, his faith has grown and matured since his college days, which I'm sure You look on as a plus instead of a minus. The tracts he left with the tip during his early adult years probably reflected his faith then, but they wouldn't reflect his enlarged grasp of what it means to be a Christian today. So if he passed out these tracts now he would be dishonest, witnessing to something he doesn't believe, and that's bad.

The obvious answer would be for him to pass around a better grade of tracts if he wants to witness to his faith, as we all should want to do. But where is he going to find religious tracts like that?

Sir, I doubt if You take the trouble to read the tracts people thrust in your hand on crowded streets, or that are left around in bus stations. If You haven't, don't bother. They are pretty bad. They are poorly written, full of bizarre theological concepts, and generally packed with misinformation about the Bible, Jesus Christ, and You. I don't doubt

CHARLES MERRILL SMITH

198

that the people who pass them out believe what's in them, but I question the evangelistic efficacy of these literary efforts. It is possible that some are saved through reading these tracts, of course, but the kind of faith they are saved to—well, as I see it, their last state would be worse than their first.

Perhaps I ought to explain that. Tractarian Christianity usually tells me that You have it in for me, but that I can escape Your wrath if I believe the right doctrines and adopt the correct religious postures. When I comply with the formula, these tracts tell me, You won't be mad at me any more, and You will allow me to escape the really bad stuff You plan to mete out to everyone who ignores the message of the tract.

You aren't actually like that, are You? If You are, then You are a sort of celestial bully. I mean, that's how the Mafia makes people do what it wants. I just can't conceive of You as a Godfather.

And if I strike the recommended religious stance in order to avoid being crocked by God, then what does that make me? Sick, that's what. If I decide to take up religion in order to beat the rap, then what I really need isn't a tract but a good psychiatrist. Salvation, if I understand the Bible correctly, is supposed to make me well. But if I follow the cure the average religious tract outlines for me, I won't get well, I'll get sicker.

I would guess that there is another reason why my friend has abandoned the distribution of religious tracts with the tip. In his maturity he probably has figured out that his motives for passing out tracts were partly bad. At the time he was spreading these leaflets here, there, and everywhere, he told himself this was a true witness, that his concern was for the salvation of others. Now he knows that he did it not entirely to save others, but partly to save himself. It was a way for him to score a lot of points in the spiritual honors competition. I'll bet he got a holy charge each time he left a tract with the tip. Back then, he didn't know he was catering to his own spiritual pride when he left that tract, but he knows it now, and that is reason enough not to do it any more.

However, I still think there is an evangelistic potential in tracts. The written word can be powerfully persuasive. I wouldn't mind at all leaving a tract with the tip if it was a first-rate tract expressing what I believe, and if I could devise a method of avoiding spiritual pride when I left it.

But I don't know where to lay hands on good, honest persuasive Christian tracts. And I haven't come up with a system for escaping spiritual pride when I leave it. When I solve these two problems I'll start leaving a tract with the tip. And I'll remember to leave a good tip with the tract.

Somehow, a penurious gratuity and an evangelistic message don't go well together.

CHARLES MERRILL SMITH

44

A Rose by Another Name Sometimes Smells Sweeter to Me

Understanding Spirit, Sir . . . I've been reading a new book on how the Christian confronts the problems of the daily grind. It is a superior book, much more real and honest than many works of this nature. But I have a problem with it. The author speckles his pages with such phrases as "commitment to Christ," and "what would Jesus have me do?" and "doing the will of Christ."

Now these are perfectly acceptable phrases, and I know that most Christians respond warmly to them. I don't, and I feel guilty because I don't. In fact, they turn me off. Though I am probably blaspheming to admit it, I feel a little queasy when someone starts talking about "God's will," or "our Heavenly Father," or "blessed Jesus."

Please don't misunderstand me. I'm not saying there is anything wrong with such talk. The problem is me. I have probed my psyche for a clue to my aversion, and have concluded that some of the trouble is traceable to early conditioning. Many of my early years were spent among what we might refer to loosely as "evangelicals," who tossed around these Jesus phrases much as other people employ the nomenclature of sports or business. I developed a distaste for this pious patois then, and I haven't been able to purge myself of it. I know this is a prejudice. It has little basis in reason or logic, and I pride myself on being a reasonable man. It is my hang-up, but I'm afraid I'm stuck with it.

On the other hand, I do not recoil from such a phrase as "Jesus is our example of what it means to be truly human," or "Jesus is God's way of showing us what life is all about." These phrases actually mean the same thing as "commitment to Christ," and to an unprejudiced ear don't sound any better. But they sound better to me. They don't make me squirm. They don't make me uncomfortable. Silly of me, isn't it?

I have one slight logical point to make in support of my prejudice. It seems to me that Jesus never wanted people to commit themselves to him. To use the biblical language, he always pointed beyond himself to You. He sought commitment to what he stood for, and to the One he represented. I have a feeling that he might not even like the idea of us calling ourselves Christians.

I find that my hang-up blocks me out from the kind of devotional life so many Christians say is so rewarding. I'm probably missing something pretty good, I know, but why try to kid myself, let alone You? I'd rather admit that devotionalism leaves me cold and take my chances than try to

CHARLES MERRILL SMITH

psych myself into believing it means something to me when it doesn't.

Sir, if You think my hang-up is bad, You're going to have to cure it, because I can't manage it myself. If You think it isn't too serious a deviation from acceptable Christian practice, then please overlook it. I can live with it if You can.

45

I Don't Want You for My Buddy

Ultimately Unknowable Spirit, Sir . . . As long as I have
been telling You about my hang-ups over Jesus language, I
might as well go on and say that I don't want You for my
buddy. This is another of my hang-ups. I know a lot of
people who derive much comfort and inspiration by thinking of You as a friendly neighbor, but I don't. I don't even
want to try.

Oh, I am aware that I have been talking to You as if You
had human attributes. But You know that I know better.
This is what the theologians call "anthropomorphizing" God,
and sometimes it is a bad thing to do, especially when we
create You in our own image to the extent of making You a
member of the American Legion, or president of the Temperance Union, or something else we are hot for. That is
for sure the sin of idolatry.

On the other hand, how am I to think of pure spirit, which You are? I have to clothe it, in my imagination, with some kind of form I can visualize. So I play this game of picturing You as a perfect human. I know it is a game, but it doesn't have to be a bad game so long as I don't confuse it with reality.

It becomes a bad game, though, when I move from picturing You in human terms to believing You are my sidekick, my best friend, a cosmic amigo who pals around with me in a special way. When I think of You in this way, which I'm always tempted to do, then I'm attempting to possess You and use You for my own benefit. If You and I had this relationship, You wouldn't be God any more. You'd be an object, an acquaintance with plenty of clout. I might like You, and enjoy Your company, and all that—but You wouldn't be the Ultimate Being any more, and sooner or later I'd be looking for an Ultimate beyond You.

So please don't be offended when I say I don't want You for my buddy. I don't want to reduce You to my size. I want You to go on being God.

Meanwhile, I'll play this game of anthropomorphizing, but I'll keep in mind that it is only a game, my method for visualizing You.

If I understand the Gospels, Jesus said that he came in order that we could have a glimpse, a clue as to what You are like.

That's enough for me.

46

Are You Bothered by Our Ways of Celebrating Christmas?

Creator of Joy, Sir . . . Every year, when Christmas rolls round, preachers fill the air with flak about the commercialization of Christ's birthday, the secularization of a sacred season, and all that. There is a lot to be said for their complaints of course. On the other hand, I have an uneasy feeling that we Christians tend to overdo our protests about leaving Christ out of Christmas.

Perhaps I can clarify my attitude by relating to You the following incident.

The pastor of the Mitzi Mayfield Memorial Church was a little late with his Christmas shopping, due to sixteen committee meetings, a denominational rally, three luncheon club addresses, and a speech for the PTA, not to mention such minor items as sermon preparation, pastoral calling, etc. He decided to begin with the names near the bottom of his list, leaving the fun part till last. So he dropped in at the Bon-Ton Men's Furnishing Emporium to pick out a few ties from the special Christmas selection ($2.50 value, only $1.98). While fingering the cravats without enthusiasm, he spied the rector of St. John's-by-the-Supermarket selecting a pair of hideous purple socks.

"Christmas shopping, eh?" said the pastor.

"Just finishing up," the rector replied.

"Thus do the clergy—me included—contribute to the commercialization of the season which we are so quick to lambast from the pulpit," the pastor said, since he was heated up on the subject, having just seen a program on the "Today" show deploring the grosser aspects of the Christmas hard sell.

"Well, I guess so," the rector said, "but, like sin and the poor, the commercialized Christmas would seem to be here to stay."

The pastor fingered a livid green tie with chartreuse zigzags and decided that it probably didn't fit his Uncle Adelbert's personality. "If the man from Mars who is going to land in a flying saucer any day now (if we can believe the UFO buffs) would happen to pop in during the Yule season, what would he make of it?" he asked the rector. "Would he be able to figure out what it's all about?"

"Probably not," the rector replied, as he snatched a fuschia silk handkerchief from a pile and added it to the purple socks. "About all he could tell from the general activity in the average American community this time of year is

HOW TO TALK TO GOD . . .

that there is a lot of rushing around with music playing in the background, the same music over and over. He'd probably be quite puzzled by it all."

"He might drop in on a church service and hear the story of Christmas," the pastor said, not very positively, as they worked their way toward the cuff links and wallet display.

"Very unlikely. But even if he did get inside a church, chances are the tinsel stars and charming mangers and cute Virgin Marys he would find in most churches would only obscure the Christmas message and confuse him the more. The churches have had a hand in devaluing the season and the story too, you know."

"So what do you propose we do about it?" the pastor asked.

"Not much of anything."

"Why not?" the pastor came back at him with some force.

"Well, for one thing, I don't get as worked up over commercialism at Christmas as some of my brethren do."

"Maybe you ought to, maybe your soul has been soiled by this sordid society, if you will forgive the alliteration," the pastor said, pleased that he had phrased it so felicitously.

"Oh, I do deplore the more crude and crass attempts to exploit our Lord's birthday in pursuit of the fast buck, but Christmas started out as a pagan holiday, you know, and the Christians appropriated it. We sometimes act as if it were the other way around. Let's be thankful for having as much of it as we have."

CHARLES MERRILL SMITH

208

"I never thought of it that way," the pastor replied, somewhat lamely.

"You ought to. Besides, we all like the secular part of the holiday—the jazzed-up atmosphere, the good will, however temporary. Say, look at this sharkskin billfold, nifty isn't it? A bit racy for a clergyman though, I suppose." He put it back regretfully. "You got any presents yet? I've already bagged a Prayer Book bound in zebra hide and a record of Oral Roberts' sermons—a long-playing record, I might add."

"I got a picture of the Last Supper that glows in the dark."

"How awful!" said the rector, and made for the items on special sale humming "God Rest Ye Merry, Gentlemen."

Sir, I pretty much identify with the rector's attitude. I'm willing to go along with some overcommercialization of the season in return for a period, however brief, in which people tend to improve their conduct, act toward one another with more compassion and consideration than is their wont, and generally make a stab at behaving as if peace, good will, and kindliness are worthwhile virtues after all. Not even the more vulgar Christmas ads or the seasonal hard sell intend disrespect toward You or a devaluation of the incarnation. And most churches do push the Christmas offering.

It would probably be better if we confined ourselves to less tawdry, more reverent ways of celebrating Christmas, but the hoopla really doesn't bother me too much, and I hope it doesn't bother You.

HOW TO TALK TO GOD . . .

47

I Believe That Sound Doctrine Will Save Me

Great Orderly Mind, Sir . . . As I address You at this moment we are in the season of general synods, national denominational conventions, biennial convocations, and all these official church conclaves by which the various sects get their business done.

Many of them, according to reports in the secular press, are wrestling with such questions as, "What is authentic Lutheran doctrine?" or "What must Baptists believe?" Not a few of the news stories emanating from these theologically troubled gatherings are written tongue in cheek, implying that the battles over dogma are much ado about nothing, and that the delegates would be better advised to quit their quibbling and get on with the important business.

I do not agree. These Christians are trying to solve the problem of what is sound Christian doctrine. And I believe that sound doctrine will save us.

For example, Sir, the Bible teaches me that whatever else You are, You are love. I take that to be sound doctrine. So long as I remain convinced that You love me I won't be uptight about life. If I know that I am loved, I won't be frantic to earn Your love, which means that I don't have to pretend to a piety I don't possess or lay claim to a righteousness which a saint couldn't sustain. I wouldn't like living under false credentials, and knowing that You love me saves me from that spiritual horror.

The Bible also teaches me that all I have to do to be saved is accept Your acceptance of me. There are no qualifying heats, no levels of moral or spiritual performance I must achieve in order to obtain Your acceptance. That is sound doctrine, and it saves me.

I really don't object, Sir, to people who go in heavily for pious postures and prefer the unctuous personality, so long as they understand that this is a matter of taste rather than doctrine, a style and not a demand You place on us. I am not much attracted to the style, but it would be just as wrong of me to say other people shouldn't strike these "religious" stances as it is if they say I must strike them or I am not saved. Some people are attracted by one style, others by some other style. But style is not what saves us.

So I applaud the efforts of the various churches to discover and reaffirm sound Christian doctrine.

The trouble is, Sir, they come up with some dumb answers.

For example, the Missouri Synod Lutherans went on record that sound doctrine prohibits the ordination of women. They signed Your name to it yet, which in my book is a blatant forgery. They claim that when St. Paul admonished the women to keep silent in the churches it was actually You speaking.

Now St. Paul was a great guy. I yield to no one in my admiration for him. But he did have his hang-ups, like all of us, and sometimes they intruded themselves in his writing. The Lutherans ought not to be blaming You for St. Paul's ideas, and You have every right to be irritated with them.

If they had said, "Well, a male-dominated society which excludes women from the priesthood is a good old German cultural custom which we Lutherans wish to perpetuate," who's to argue? I mean, the Lutherans have every right to dictate what Lutherans shall and shall not do. But they shouldn't call it sound Christian doctrine.

It seems to me, Sir, that too many of Your servants, seeking to determine what is sound Christian doctrine, end up by including far too much in their list. There is something in us which longs to dot all the i's and cross all the t's of faith, tie it up in a package, answer every possible question. Theologians of any brand have this weakness.

Maybe they are right, but faith isn't any fun that way. Living the life of faith when faith provides a specific answer for every question is like following a doctor's prescribed regimen, or living forever on a diet. It is similar to the routine an airline pilot goes through in his preflight checklist.

Personally, I don't want faith reduced to a formula. I want it to be open-ended. It has to have possibilities that doctrinal experts can't envision. It has to have answers to questions no one has asked yet, but will have to ask as the conditions

CHARLES MERRILL SMITH

of life change and the shape of things to come become apparent.

So, while I believe sound doctrine will save me, too much doctrine can foul up the life of faith.

Anyway, Sir, this is where I stand on the issue, and I don't think the devil made me do it.

48

I Need a Shot of the Gambler's Spirit

Sir . . . Are You against gambling?

What brought the question to mind is a story I read in the
paper about an English preacher. He proposed to solve his
parish financial problems by encouraging his parishioners
to put a couple of bob, or even a quid if they could afford it,
on the ponies, then turn over their winnings to the church.

The story doesn't tell us how he came to think up this scheme,
but it isn't hard to imagine how he did it.

What probably happened was that one wet, chilly English
evening the good vicar was huddled before the fireplace
(Why do the English persist in rejecting central heating?)
in his vast and drafty rectory, with his New Testament on
one knee and the parish financial summary on the other.

214

The financial summary, no doubt, was as gloomy as the weather.

So he began thumbing through the Gospels for comfort, in the process of which he came across the parable of the talents. He had been pondering the depressing axiom, known to all parish pastors, that Christians are reluctant to contribute enough money to their churches to keep them going. He read the familiar words relating how the master, in Jesus' story, handed out money to three of his servants and told them to go out and make some money with it.

Maybe some variation of this scheme is what we need in this parish, the vicar mused, but I'd better work up a new angle, sort of modernize it. Maybe, he reflected, I ought to combine the idea of the parable with something people like to do anyway.

At this point, all the various strands of thought came together. The great white light of revelation illumined him, and leaping from his chair with a high-decibel shout which alarmed his wife and startled the vicarage cat, he exclaimed, "Eureka! I'll have them gamble!"

So the next Sunday, to prime the pump and get the project off the ground in approved biblical fashion, he distributed fifty pounds (about one hundred twenty dollars at the current rate of exchange) to his congregation. Go and gamble for the Lord, he instructed, and bring your winnings to church next Sunday.

It is incidental to the point I want to make, Sir, but the vicar's scheme sent my imagination racing. I spent too many years raising the annual church budget, and it was always a drag. Doing it the vicar's way, though, ought to be fun.

In the first place, it ought to work like a charm. People obviously like gambling better than they like putting money in the collection plate. If people could gamble and feel pious about it, who would refrain?

We American Christians, with our good old American know-how, could improve on the vicar's imaginative stewardship program.

Each denomination would want to phase out its board of Christian stewardship and replace it with a national agency to promote godly gambling. They could call it the Board of Christian Talent Investment, or some variation of this name, because church boards need melifluous and euphemistic names, especially ones which exist for the purpose of raising money.

The board would need to publish a weekly magazine which should be a three- or four-color tip sheet on where the conscientious layman could get his weekly wager down at the best obtainable odds. The tip sheet would cost money, but it could be financed out of the savings from the abandonment of special denominational offerings. Special offerings cost plenty for promotional material—special envelopes, mailing, etc. Under the vicar's plan, these offerings would not be needed.

A local church with any get up and go would want to organize a Fellowship of the Holy Horseplayers. This fellowship would meet to study how, when, where, and how much to wager for the best results, then inform the congregation.

There would be possibilities in a weekly Pious Pool on upcoming sporting events such as the World Series or the Super

CHARLES MERRILL SMITH

216

Bowl. I even thought of a pool in which the church could sell all the numbers in the hymnal each week, then the people holding the numbers of the hymns sung each Sunday would collect (which would have as a spin-off a marked increase of interest in hymn singing). However, since the pastor normally picks the hymns, this would subject him to pressures and temptations it is best for a pastor to avoid. So maybe it isn't such a hot idea.

Don't take me too seriously, Sir, because it is doubtful if the vicar's plan will catch on. It's a gimmick, and anyway we American Christians are prejudiced against gambling. But the way the parable of the talents comes out, there is no arguing—the moral is that we should have some gambling spirit in the way we confront life. The guys who gambled with their talents earned the master's approval, and the one who played it safe got smacked down pretty hard.

I really have no doubts about the parable of the talents. I feel certain that Jesus is saying that we ought to live with a sort of holy recklessness, lay our lives on the line, bet a bundle on You. I am by no means the first to interpret the parable this way. In fact, there isn't much of any other way to read it.

The trouble is, Sir, it goes against something in my nature. I never did get any fun or excitement out of gambling. Some people do, but I don't. I prefer a sure thing. I'm the kind of fellow who always hedges his bets, frets about the outcome, hates to lose. I have to be pushed into bold and chancy decisions and action by circumstances. I admire people like Columbus and Grenfell and the astronauts, and I wish I could be one of those daring spirits. But the truth is, I prefer security.

And I'm getting more timid, less venturesome about life as my arteries harden and I count the years until I will be on Social Security. I'm pretty certain about You, of course, but even You are no sure thing.

I need a shot of the gambler's spirit. The good vicar's plan for church finance is a crazy scheme, but it isn't as unchristian as it seems at first glance. The basic idea is consistent with Christian teaching about the nature of our life.

I guess I'll go read the parable of the talents again. Maybe it will give me the spiritual hypo that I know I need.

CHARLES MERRILL SMITH

49

I'm Still Not Feeling Religious

Ultimate Reality, Sir . . . I began these conversations with You precisely because I wasn't feeling religious and wanted to say some things which will never be included in a prayer book or a devotional manual. I wish to reiterate that none of these communications have been sent up in a spirit of irreverence. I didn't feel irreverent; I just didn't feel religious. I still don't.

I'm not sure that I can explain the difference between not feeling irreverent but not feeling religious. The kind of Christianity with which I am best acquainted has always put a premium on feeling religious. Sir, if You knew the times I have gone to church, or participated in a devotional service round a campfire or someplace, and nearly everyone got turned on by the religious current flowing, and I didn't, You'd know what I am trying to make plain.

Truth to tell, I didn't even know what I was supposed to feel —holy, or goosebumpy, or choked up, or exhilarated, or what. Whatever it was, I was apparently insulated from it.

I have no criticism of those who find it easy to feel religious. Matter of fact, I rather envy them, just as I frequently envy the phlegmatic personality who never suffers mood swings as I do. I think it would be grand to get zipped up for the Lord or have a high old time to Your glory.

So, Sir, it's not that I think feeling religious and showing it is undignified or in bad taste. Dignity and good taste are overrated virtues anyway. It's just that it isn't my nature to have mystical experiences or jump for joy in my religion. I expect I'm pretty inhibited.

For a long time I felt guilty about this. I was rather certain that, at best, I was only lingering around the outer suburbs of faith, that I had never been downtown. I even believed the ill-informed preaching which told me that if I didn't feel it I didn't have it.

Well, Sir, I may be a junior-grade Christian because I seldom feel religious. But I have come to discover that there are plenty of others who are in the same boat with me. And I can't believe that You are going to sink the boat because of our inhibitions or psychological inadequacies.

In my own defense let me state that I am not devoid of feelings.

I am often filled to overflowing with a sense of gratitude toward You for the gift of creation and the joy of being alive. There is no sense in which I have feelings of fear

CHARLES MERRILL SMITH

toward You. What I feel toward You can best be described as grateful respect.

Also, I can feel something tremendous, something beyond description in, say, Durham Cathedral (Do You have a preference for Norman Gothic as I do?), or viewing Michelangelo's *David*. That's an esthetic feeling, which I would think should be classed as religious. But it isn't what religious people mean when they speak of feeling religious.

Well, Sir, I'm so glad You made it clear in the Bible that I am saved by my faith and not by my feelings. Some Christians probably have considerably more religious fun than I do, but that doesn't mean that I have to have spiritual inferiority feelings.

I genuinely appreciate the fact, Sir, that You apparently are tolerant of so many different personality types. As I get it, You do not insist that we must all be identical in our religious experience. Perhaps it would be wise for You to emphasize this point to the various Christian sects and denominations, because nearly all of them want to process their members and turn them out like Fords, all alike. I believe this pressure for spiritual conformity to be one of the worst sins of denominational Christianity.

So I am going to plod along at the business of living out my faith without benefit of mandates from bishops, direction from spiritual-life secretaries, or processing by denominational program. I know I would be more comfortable if I said, "Oh, what the heck, these leaders are smarter than I am, they ought to know what God wants of me, so I'll just go along with what they say and quit worrying about relating my faith to the world."

But Sir, I want to worry about it. Or rather, I don't want to be a Christian mechanical man, and the only way I can avoid that is to worry about it. I will make mistakes, both in thought and in deed, as I'm sure You know. But they will be my mistakes, and maybe I'll learn something from them. That will make them a much better grade of mistakes than if I were only doing what someone else told me to do.

You, of course, are a fixed point in the constellation of my convictions. So is Jesus.

I don't know much about You, to be sure. You are the creator of this good world. You love it, and You love me. You love me, not because of what I am, but in spite of it. You will bring in Your kingdom in Your own good time. I can't be positive, but I'm pretty sure that this event will take place beyond history, not within it. But that's Your worry, not mine.

And that's about all I know about You. But that is enough. If You don't mind, I'm not going to get bogged down in defending the doctrine of the Holy Trinity or the Nicene Creed. The doctrine of the Holy Trinity is a very nice doctrine, and the Nicene Creed, an estimable document. They provide endless opportunity for speculation and theological debate for people who like that sort of thing. That's fine, but it isn't my bag.

What I find continually fascinating is the examination and reexamination of what Jesus means for us today. For me, he is an inexhaustible source of direction, inspiration, and information of what life is all about. I believe he is Your statement of what You expect from me.

Sir, I'm not putting it very well, and my faith in Jesus Christ

CHARLES MERRILL SMITH